P9-ASN-170

No-Fault

NO-FAULT

What You Save, Gain, and Lose
with the New Auto Insurance

PAUL GILLESPIE
and
MIRIAM KLIPPER

PRAEGER PUBLISHERS
New York • Washington • London

PRAEGER PUBLISHERS
111 Fourth Avenue, New York, N.Y. 10003, U.S.A.
5, Cromwell Place, London SW7 2JL, England

Published in the United States of America in 1972
by Praeger Publishers, Inc.

Library of Congress Catalog Card Number: 73–184337

Printed in the United States of America

To Elizabeth and Nathaniel

Contents

No-Fault

I

After Keeton-O'Connell

THE MAGNITUDE OF WHAT has become an automobile insurance crisis is clearly demonstrated by statistics. At present, there are over 100 million licensed motor vehicle operators in the United States, driving more than 100 million registered motor vehicles. The drivers and these vehicles travel approximately 1 trillion miles per year and are involved in over 14 million motor vehicle collisions. Aside from the physical damage done to property, the human loss is appalling.

The National Safety Council recently announced 2 million separate personal injury claims arising out of automobile accidents. In 1971, over 60,000 lives were sacrificed on U.S. highways. In order to pay for the cost of these accidents, the insurance industry writes an amount approaching $6 billion in automobile casualty insurance. Because of the sheer volume of accidents, the enormous dollar amount expended to finance claims, and the high price of premiums, an intensive search is now under way to find more efficient ways of compensating the survivors while cutting the costs of automobile insurance.

Out front in the movement for automobile insurance reform is the no-fault device. No-fault insurance—or collect from your company, no matter who is at fault—is becoming a nationwide drive. This major challenge to soaring automobile insurance rates abandons established principles of civil law and creates a new legal relationship: man versus his insurance company in place of driver versus driver.

In theory, no-fault automobile insurance would replace the traditional method of compensating automobile accident injuries—in which the victim makes a claim directly against an individual wrongdoer or, in reality, the wrongdoer's insurance company—with a more direct relationship. The victim now makes a claim for damages to his own company, instead of turning to his opponent's. The question of who is negligent or at fault is dropped from the legal dialogue.

According to insurance industry spokesmen, the relationship between policyholder and company under no-fault would be indentical to that which exists under a homeowner's or life insurance policy, known in industry parlance as first-party coverage. The adversary system emphasizing negligence would be replaced by a contractual relationship. Two parties, the insurance company and the car owner, enter into a written contract to fix the payment of damages in advance. This protection is extended to the car owner, members of his family, the driver, and occupants of the car, as well as pedestrians struck by that car.

Though there is no single standard form of no-fault automobile insurance, most states are expected to adopt some kind of plan, and a national no-fault plan is a strong possibility. Because of this diversity, it is impossible to make sweeping statements that would be valid for all cases; yet no-fault plans have certain common characteristics.

Basically, these plans seek to eliminate the court system as a forum for the settlement of claims arising out of automobile accidents, which the proponents of no-fault argue create court congestion and waste money and time. As other targets, no-fault plans seek a reduction in claim volume, an end to the need to exaggerate injuries, the elimination of fraud, quick and efficient methods of payment directly to the accident victim, and a better distribution of the insurance premium dollar. It has been estimated that as much as 56 per cent of the premium dollar is consumed by overhead before any money is paid to the victim. This figure, if correct, shows a need for drastic overhaul of the entire insurance system.

No one would argue with these general objectives of reform. But how the consumer can benefit from no-fault is less clear. Though it is believed as an article of faith by its advocates that more of the premium dollar will be returned to the accident victim and less will go to the administration and other costs of running a fault system, this belief is somewhat difficult to substantiate. At present, there is only a sparse amount of data on expense and loss experience with no-fault plans. Secondly, although legal costs are reduced, or in some plans virtually eliminated, the total number of individuals eligible to make claims is sharply increased over what was possible under a fault system. This dramatic increase in potential claim volume may escalate rather than reduce costs, even without resort to the courts. Because all victims are eligible for benefits, beneficiaries may increase by as much as 50 per cent. To accommodate the cost problem, therefore, the temptation is ever present to shrink no-fault benefits.

The situation is complicated by another possibility. We may find that the best arrangement would be a hybrid fault–no-fault system. This would combine the advantage of immediate compensation from the victim's own insurance company with the opportunity to pursue claims involving more serious injuries by taking the more extreme case to the courts. How much of the premium dollar would find its way back into the consumer's pocket is uncertain. The answer will depend heavily upon the extent to which claims continue to be made under the traditional fault system.

Because reform is moving at a rapid pace, there is an urgent need to identify the correct place at which a no-fault system which is beneficial for minor cases should convert to a fault system for more serious injuries. The public not only bears the cost of insurance, but also suffers the consequences as victims, and must ultimately insist that equities be preserved. Virtually all no-fault proponents thus far have conceded that there are severe cases that demand the retention of fault and the right to full compensation. The most significant question we can ask at this stage is: How will the various reforms alter the present law of compensation for damages?

In the past, an automobile accident victim who could prove that his injury was caused by the negligence of another was entitled to collect the full amount for his damages, including compensation for medical expenses, loss of earning capacity, pain and suffering, disfigurement, emotional upset, and any other incidental damages. No-fault severely restricts the possibility of full recovery in virtually all cases and is designed to compensate only medical expenses and a percentage of actual lost earnings, omitting claims for such well-established damages as loss of bodily function, scarring, and emotional upset.

At the heart of the no-fault dilemma is this simple problem. In order to pay everyone injured in an automobile accident something, benefits must be taken away from the innocent victim, who under a fault system would be compensated fully and fairly. By eliminating full compensation including pain and suffering in the majority of cases, the cost of insurance can be significantly reduced.

There is another critical judgment to be made before transforming the law to no-fault. Are we not losing the benefit of judges and juries and their ability to tailor justice to each individual case? In awarding damages under common law, a judge or jury is permitted a high degree of flexibility. Whatever the shortcomings of the negligence system, it cannot be called insensitive to the ideal of fairness to the individual. No-fault damages, on the other hand, are parceled out on a rigid, structured, and objective basis; because everyone has a right to be compensated, damages are restricted to economic losses and are reduced to a fraction of what they might have been under common-law principles. Before the public embraces the no-fault cause, let it understand that costs may be reduced, but certain valuable rights will be discarded in the process.

Although the elimination of fault-finding and its usual companion, the drawn-out battle in the courts, leads to a certain efficiency, what is missing in the current public debate is a fuller examination of what will replace the court system if it is no longer used to decide accident litigation. Because everyone is a potential accident victim, the implications of abandoning traditional ways of receiving compensation for injuries ought not to be taken lightly. That the courts are congested in a few metropolitan areas is true, but this cannot be made the basis for saying that automobile accident cases have no right being there. The effort now should be directed toward identifying the point at which a lawsuit is unworthy of being present in our court system. It is one thing to bruise a leg, but it is another to lose it entirely.

We must ask ourselves: Do we really want to put a price tag on justice? Do we want to pay for a system that will provide a legal method that both fully compensates injuries and balances equities? The insuring public must insist that any new insurance law be more than expedient, efficient, and less expensive.

Essentially a system of no-fault insurance widens the circle around those eligible for payment, and, by so doing, it protects a greater number of people. How far this circle should be extended is a question of policy. Advocates of no-fault insurance say that accidents are unavoidable: They constitute a part of the price of driving an automobile, and the risk ought to be spread among all those who pay insurance premiums. Since all consumers are potential victims, anyone injured in an automobile accident should be compensated at least to a limited extent. But to accomplish this, and keep the price within reason, the careful driver has to take less. To make no-fault acceptable, the drafters of the various plans have indulged in what may be called the fiction of the nuisance claim.

Although the no-fault pattern is not uniform, these plans have as a stated goal the elimination of 80–90 per cent of the automobile accident claims currently determined and paid for by the law of negligence. Is it conceivable that 80 per cent to 90 per cent of the claims now filed are in fact mere nuisance claims? At what point does it become socially desirable to classify a particular injury as small or serious and to depart from fault standards into no-fault? To date, this line has not been well drawn.

The "cost-equity" dilemma of automobile insurance—or where do you draw the line between savings to the consumer and justice for the injured—has been tackled by two professors of law, Robert Keeton, of the Harvard Law School, and Jeffrey O'Connell, of the College of Law, University of Illinois. Their plan, which first appeared in 1965, belongs in any discussion of contemporary no-fault insurance. It received wide attention then; ever since, it has been a model for all no-fault plans, though it has never been adopted and it is unlikely that it ever will be. The plan is a combination of no-fault coverage and traditional negligence liability. Keeton and O'Connell designed a proposal to compensate all traffic accident victims for economic losses up to a limit of $10,000, regardless of fault. In exchange for this $10,000 worth of economic protection, the victim loses the right to sue the wrongdoer for damages that exceed his economic loss, except for catastrophic cases.

Suppose that a driver, while stopped at a red light, is struck violently from behind by another driver. The wrongdoer admits the accident is his fault and apologizes. Both are injured to the same extent. The driver who was blameless in the accident suffers a financial loss, through a combination of medical bills and salary loss, of $1,000. The second driver's losses are the same. The Keeton-O'Connell plan would pay both $1,000. It would pay nothing to the first for any pain and suffering or any other general damages that he would have received under a fault system; these damages might have been worth several hundred dollars. The negligent driver, who would receive nothing under a fault system, obtains the same amount as the first, despite the fact that he caused the accident. In effect, the good driver has lost benefits he would have received under a fault system in order to pay economic damages to the bad driver.

Keeton and O'Connell stress that the effort to determine who is at fault is a luxury that the automobile compensation system cannot afford. Instead of allocating money to fault-finding, they prefer to see this saving go directly to all victims, even to those who cause injury to themselves and to others.

The Keeton-O'Connell bill imposes a limit to economic damages that can be recovered. The reason is simple economics: The cost of premiums for a no-fault system without a ceiling on the amount of compensation would be considerably more expensive than a system that imposed a maximum amount. The other reason for a ceiling is tied to the problem of equity. Serious injuries demand compensation beyond economic reimbursement. Keeton and O'Connell, while recognizing equity in theory, ignore it in practice, because their threshold of $10,000 prevents innumerable victims from being fully compensated for serious injuries.

The no-fault method, useful for dealing with small claims —those claims for which there is no severe or permanent injury and for which the economic loss is the greatest part of the claim—becomes less desirable as the amount of pain and suffering increases. For example, in the case of a man who has lost a limb in a traffic accident, to compensate him solely for wages and medical fees is grossly unfair. The same would be true of a victim who lost his eyesight or who had a permanent and disfiguring scar or a woman who suffered a miscarriage.

When it comes to the small claim, by limiting compensation to economic losses, no-fault fits the bill. Why burden the adversary system with a small case when the cost of the fight often exceeds the amount of the claim? Most anyone would admit it is better expending money for benefits to the victim as opposed to financing a small claims battle.

In an effort to keep costs low, the original Keeton-O'Connell plan and its offspring also become parasites on other institutions and groups. Under these plans, automobile insurance becomes secondary protection for compensating

automobile accident victims; the policyholder is required
first to exhaust all his collateral sources before using automobile coverage. In the case of an employee covered by a
company plan that continues paying wages during his in-
capacity, the company in which that person is employed is
in effect paying the cost of traffic accidents. Automobile insurance receives an indirect subsidy by not having to pay its
own way. The same may be said for a victim who is insured
under a private health insurance plan. He must first use up
his coverage. This means that medical claims arising from
automobile accidents place an additional strain on an already overburdened medical insurance system. Yet, without
these subtractions for private collateral resources, the cost
of no-fault plans become too high. What we have is an artificial cost-saving device resulting in illusory reductions.

Suppose a wage earner is injured in an automobile accident. Through his union, he has a wage-continuation plan
and medical coverage, which his union bargained for as a
substitute for more money in his pay envelope. When he goes
to his insurance company, he is told to look first to his union
benefits. He is understandably confused, because he thought
he had paid his insurance premiums. Because of this cost-
shifting, he is forced to pay twice.

The original Keeton-O'Connell plan and its successors can
be salvaged only if two things happen. First, the cost-equity
gap must be closed to a point where serious injury is rede-
fined to give those who are severely injured, in addition to
the no-fault economic benefits, full, adequate, and just compensation for all their damages. Second, the parasitical ef-
fects must be eliminated and automobile insurance forced to
pay its own way. Since the no-fault automobile insurance
debate began, far too much attention has been paid to the
cost side of the equation and not nearly enough to the
equities. While it is true that the organized bar has resisted

the concept of no-fault insurance, it must also be pointed out in fairness that it has been the most vocal force defending the equity part of the cost-equity balance. The public, when it makes a decision on no-fault insurance, must consider the equity factor with the same fervor as costs. Unfortunately, equity is hard to conceptualize for the man paying his insurance bill. It is difficult to talk about fractures, amputations, or scars in the abstract, while it is easy to calculate costs savings, particularly when it is agreed that automobile insurance premiums are far too high.

To now personal injury protection has occupied the spotlight. Since two out of every three dollars expended in automobile casualty insurance is spent on property damage, if any sensible no-fault system is to be established, it must include compulsory property damage coverage as well. Unlike personal injury protection, where some elements of damage are intangible, property damages can be easily and objectively computed. The majority of property damage cases are small and, as a practical matter, should not be the subject of lawsuits in the volumes they are now generating. It is recognized that many of the abuses present in the fault system have grown out of the insurance industry policy of handling property damage claims in a slow and arbitrary manner.

Because the maximum loss exposure—the amount of the property damage—is known, many companies have used the fault system to beat down a claimant to a percentage of his loss in the hope that the company by its superior financial position will be able to outlast the man with the damaged fender. The system has been frustratingly slow. Before parting with any money, the company, in addition to requiring liability reports from the insured, the claimant, witnesses, and sometimes the police, will often require an on-the-scene appraisal. It is commonly two, three, or more months before the case is resolved. The situation is unpleasant enough when an innocent driver must operate his car in a damaged condition, but it is intolerable when he is totally deprived of the use of his car for so long a time. Americans love their cars dearly, and nothing has brought the fault system into greater disfavor than the manner in which property damage claims have been mishandled. The introduction of compulsory property damage coverage would also eliminate the practice of protecting a property damage claim by filing a personal injury claim along with it to ensure proper attention.

One of the strong points of the Keeton-O'Connell basic protection plan is the so-called double-option property damage coverage, which would put property damage on a no-fault basis. When you dent someone else's fender, the driver who suffers the damage goes to his own company for recovery. Despite the insurance industry's support of no-fault insurance as it applies to personal injury cases, it has been curiously slow to respond to the question of no-fault property damage. The reason may well lie in the fact that the companies are now collecting two premiums for property damage: One is physical damage protection designed to cover losses by hitting someone else's car, and the second coverage is collision protection for the insured to pay for damage to his own vehicle. An inference might be drawn that the insurance industry is far happier with the present setup, which permits two separate premiums, than it would be with one no-fault billing. Property damage coverage should be compulsory; and it should be no-fault. Since no-fault automobile insurance is experimental, the safer course would be to first apply this principle to property damage coverage. If it fails, it fails to protect property losses and not human lives.

So far, the no-fault argument has been confined to automobile insurance reform. A broader question may be raised: Why concentrate our efforts only on those individuals injured in automobile accidents? Why not compensate victims of all types of illnesses and accidents under one plan? It is anomalous to protect only those people who by sheer chance are injured while engaged in an activity centered around an automobile. The no-fault approach, brought to its logical conclusion, would seem headed toward a system of total protection against all economic losses regardless of the cause. The time may be approaching when the federal government will operate a national no-fault injury and illness protection plan. But until that day arrives, the search for an adequate automobile insurance reform must continue in earnest.

2
Shaw's Law

UP TO THE PRESENT, automobile casualty insurance has acted as a device to supplement the law by providing protection for wrongdoers, compensating victims, and spreading accident risks by limiting the costs that might fall on any one individual. Because insurance has traditionally taken a back seat to law, the industry feels burdened by outmoded restraints. The doctrine of negligence, for example, first came to the legal forefront in the early years of the Industrial Revolution as an umbrella to protect employers from being sued by workers injured on the job. This stratagem of fault-finding has survived to dominate automobile insurance. In the opinion of the reformers, fault and automobile insurance are mismatched; no-fault must now bring law into harmony with insurance.

Under the guise of controlling the costs of premiums and providing better service, the insurance companies are busy trying to promote changes that will reverse the roles of law and insurance. Where formerly insurance writers were content to protect against payment of damages imposed by the law of negligence by having to place blame, the companies now want to break away and reshape the law to their own advantage. The fault system, because it is adversary, rates the policyholder for his potential to harm others. Consequently, losses are difficult to predict, there are no contractual restraints on the person making the claim, including the threat to cancel, and due to the need for investigation and defense, overhead costs are high.

As Herbert S. Denenberg, insurance commissioner of Pennsylvania, put it, "There have been widespread attempts on the part of the insurance industry to find a neatly packageable risk." They seek a risk that is easy to prove and that, at the same time, predicts losses and controls the claims volume. Let the consumer beware: The main issue of automobile insurance reform is not simply fault versus no-fault but to discourage attempts on the part of the insurance industry to tailor the law to fit its own economic interest.

Whether fault or no-fault prevails answers only part of the question. The other and more important point is payment for injuries. How is the amount of compensation now being offered to accident victims going to be affected by the legal about-face of automobile insurance? The word fault itself inaccurately describes the common-law basis of compensating damages. The use of the word implies a moral judgment, but fault (when used in connection with the concept of being negligent) simply means the failure of an individual to act with that degree of care required by the law to protect other persons.

The U.S. system of accident compensation stems directly from law in use in Great Britain at the time America was colonized. Its origins go deep into Anglo-Saxon history. Because of the absence of early records, opinions differ as to how the British system of law originated, though it is generally agreed it developed as an expedient method of peace-keeping, for some kind of social device was needed to discourage the violent feuds that characterized medieval society. In place of anarchy, or of resorting to self-help, a fixed method of compensating victims developed into what became the law of torts, the seed from which automobile insurance later grew.

A tort is a civil wrong recognized by the law and for which the law is willing to compensate a victim in the form of money. It differs from criminal law. A tort is a private matter between individuals, whereas a criminal offense is committed against the state, although in the early days of common law there were no clear-cut distinctions between a tort and a crime. For example, violation of a traffic law is a crime, whereas an accident due to this violation causing injury to another is a tort. The same act can be both a tort and a crime, but the consequences for the wrongdoer differ.

Early torts were not concerned with fault. The law at that time was more interested in finding the cause of an injury than placing blame on the wrongdoer. It did not ask whether an individual was careless or negligent or even intentionally wrong but only sought a connection between an act and an injury. The automobile insurance shift from basing liability on fault to strict liability or no-fault is thus a return to an earlier tradition—compensation for damages regardless of fault.

It was not until late in the development of common law that the concept of fault or moral responsibility took its place as an issue in the law of torts. As the distinction between civil and criminal law sharpened, emphasis on the defendant's fault as a basis for holding him blameworthy was adopted by criminal law, but, in civil cases, the question of fault did not come up until the early nineteenth century. Early torts were not subtle; the overwhelming number committed were direct, violent, and usually fatal. Indirect torts, the other type of tort liability that evolved, were also based on liability without fault, and were designed to compensate victims for injuries indirectly caused by a breach of duty associated with particular occupations. A coachman who, neglecting to repair a wheel, caused injury to a traveler could be sued.

In both intentional and unintentional torts, an attempt was made to place responsibility on an individual and hold him accountable to the injured victim for the damages. But it was never necessary for the injured to prove specifically how the damage happened or who was at fault. Alongside the law of liability, there was a parallel growth in the law of damages; compensation for the victim was a prime concern. There was a distinct effort on the part of the early court system to fully compensate the injured in all cases and for all damage done to him.

Modern law, producing the law of negligence on which automobile insurance is based, took shape after the first quarter of the nineteenth century. Several reasons are offered for the late debut of the tort of negligence—the most sound, that, as a social device, it was unneeded prior to the Industrial Revolution. In an unmechanized, relatively uncomplicated, and rural society, there were few occasions when forces could combine to result in an accident due to someone else's negligent act.

The pivotal case in the origin of the law of negligence—the landmark 1850 Massachusetts decision of *Brown* v. *Kendall*—which did so much to assist the growth of capitalism, ironically rose out of a dogfight. Two dog-owners, ultimately the plaintiff and defendant, stood by while their dogs fought. When the fight went too far, one of the owners picked up a stick and tried to separate the dogs. In the process, the defendant stepped back and inadvertently struck the other owner, the plaintiff, in the eye. Under the common-law principles of that time, the plaintiff could be compensated without any further proof except that the injury was directly caused, but the court in this case departed from established principles to break new ground. The great Chief Justice of the Supreme Judicial Court of Massachusetts Lemuel Shaw wrote the decision:

> If it appeared that the defendant was doing a lawful act, that is, breaking up the fight, and unintentionally hit and hurt the plaintiff, then unless it also appears to the satisfaction of the jury that the defendant is chargeable with some fault, negligence, carelessness, or want of prudence . . . the plaintiff fails to sustain the proof and is not entitled to recover.

With these words, the common law made the historic shift from strict liability, or no-fault, to fault. The implication of the *Brown* v. *Kendall* decision spread rapidly throughout the United States and to Great Britain, and the law of negligence came to supersede the theory of strict liability. Any case thereafter involving accidental injury was brought to court as an action of tort for negligence.

A second great principle molding negligence law grew out of the case of *Vaughn* v. *Menlove*, which created the doctrine of the reasonable man, a mythical person to whose behavior all conduct is legally compared. The individual was no longer judged by what he himself was capable of doing relative to his age or physical condition or mentality. The test of the reasonable man set up an external standard, and the defendant's conduct was judged against what would have been expected of a prudent individual confronted by an identical set of circumstances. The test of the reasonable man still has its place in the law of negligence. To measure whether or not a particular driver was negligent in an accident, his actions are compared to the standard of the reasonable man.

The development of negligence as a method of collecting damages in the nineteenth century was a successful effort on the part of the courts to assist the emerging industrial society in ridding itself of restraints imposed by the existing tort system. The requirement of first having to prove fault in a case helped the entrepreneur by limiting the number of people who could win lawsuits against him. Once the tort of negligence was grafted, it became necessary for the plaintiff to show how he had been injured and that the injury was, in fact, caused by fault or neglect on the part of the person injuring him.

Suppose a man is struck by a train and is seriously injured. Prior to the development of the law of negligence, he would have sued the railroad successfully, by showing that his injury had been directly caused by the train striking him. This was the only proof required. He did not have to show fault or negligence, only that he was hit and was injured. After *Brown* v. *Kendall,* because of having to prove fault, he was forced to offer a higher degree of proof; he had to produce evidence that the railroad was in some way negligent in permitting an unsafe condition to exist for an unreasonable length of time, and that this led to the accident.

As society grew increasingly complex, it became economically desirable to institute still more restrictive methods of establishing fault. So that technology and enterprise could prosper, the law made a choice and identified certain risks it considered acceptable even if these risks caused injury or loss of life. If there was to be "progress"—if steel mills were to be built and railroads were to run—the law could not hold responsible everyone causing injury in the course of economic activity. As proving negligence became a precondition for recovery, the circle around the number of people who could recover for injuries tightened. Because it was costly to compensate all those who were either directly or indirectly injured by a particular enterprise, the theory of liability with fault or negligence prospered.

Not only did the law insist on proof of fault, but also it looked to the conduct of the victim himself to measure whether he was worthy of compensation. Had he, through his own careless action, contributed to the injury? Restrictive doctrines of "contributory negligence" and "assumption of the risk," which later played a major role in automobile insurance, served to reduce further the number of plaintiffs who could recover in civil lawsuits. Aside from compelling the plaintiff to show that the defendant had caused his injury, contributory negligence placed upon the plaintiff the added burden of proving that he had in no way contributed to his own injury. Were the plaintiff responsible for as little as 1 per cent of this injury, he could not recover even against the most careless defendant.

"Assumption of the risk" shut out recovery, particularly in industrial cases. It meant that the plaintiff, having voluntarily assumed the risk of undertaking a hazardous job or other activity, waived his right to claim damages when injured. Returning to the man struck by the train, the plaintiff had to prove that the railroad was at fault, that he did not in any way contribute to his injury by his own carelessness, and that he did not assume the risk of his injury by walking too near the tracks. As pitfalls were placed in the path of the injured plaintiff, legal concern for the welfare of the victim was transferred to concern for the wrongdoer. This trend away from strict liability to negligence continued throughout the nineteenth century and into the twentieth.

No-fault made its comeback with the concept of workmen's compensation. Ten states first passed workmen's compensation laws in 1911, and, by the 1950's, all states had followed suit. Although it is commonly believed that workmen's compensation statutes were passed solely for the protection of the workingman, the employer gained advantages as well. He received immunity from common-law suits by purchasing insurance to protect himself against employee injuries. The benefits under workmen's compensation were a small fraction of the amount the victim might have recovered earlier. As in the case of no-fault automobile insurance, noneconomic losses such as pain and suffering were excluded.

No-fault automobile insurance has often been compared to workmen's compensation coverage, another form of no-fault. It is based on the principle that the cost of industrial accidents should be part of the total cost of doing business, just as the cost of compensating accident victims should be made part of the total cost of driving. Personal injuries are absorbed into the social price of the activity, in much the same way that accident payments are reflected in the cost of insurance to every motorist.

But there are also great differences in the two systems. Before workmen's compensation was passed, if a man lost an arm in the course of his employment, it was unlikely that he would receive any compensation. The law at that time was heavily weighted in favor of the employer, who could say that the hazards of the job were well known to the worker beforehand. The worker was on the job voluntarily and at his own risk, with the result that most cases went unpaid. Also the worker had to prove his employer was negligent. As a practical matter, many employees, particularly before the unions were strong, were not about to lose their jobs by striking out against their employer, who would resent being taken to court. In short, the atmosphere surrounding the passage of workmen's compensation was considerably different from the present controversy over no-fault automobile insurance.

In the case of the fault automobile insurance system, protection was available to a high percentage of motorists. The outcry for no-fault reform did not come from those people who lost automobile accident lawsuits. It came from the government, the insurance industry, and the academic community.

But a more important point by far is that, under workmen's compensation, the employee could still retain his common-law rights to sue for negligence by asking that, when he began work, they could be made part of the employment bargain. Although this rarely happened, it does show a deep regard for the validity of common-law rights in the face of what at the time was revolutionary and radical legislation. As we will see, the right to sue for fundamental damages is missing from virtually all no-fault automobile insurance proposals.

Aside from workmen's compensation, no-fault or strict liability has also been imposed in situations where the loss is so catastrophic that evidence disappears along with the accident; airplane crashes, atomic-reactor blowdowns, and other extra-hazardous activities involving the use of explosives illustrate the point. There are generally no survivors, and negligence or fault becomes a moot point. Because of this, instead of denying recovery altogether, for want of proof, the courts in recent years have done away with placing blame.

The same no-fault approach has taken over the field of products liability. The plaintiff, because he is so far removed from the negligent act, would find it impossible to prove that a manufacturer, carrier, or retailer was in fact responsible. Again, we have a shift in traditional principles of law. Earlier, a manufacturer was liable for a product that caused damage if there was a contract of sale—the purchase of goods by a buyer from a seller. Otherwise, the injured person was left with the impossible task of proving that the manufacturer was negligent. A person hurt in an accident caused by a defective product had to prove he was the purchaser. If some innocent third person were injured, he could not be compensated, because he was not a party to the sale, and, as a result, very few product-liability injuries were compensated at all.

The shortcomings of this approach are obvious. Recently, in a number of innovative decisions, many courts have radically departed from the old contractual theory of product liability. The California Supreme Court held that, particularly in cases involving major industries, contractual obligation as a precondition to recovery was outdated and unfair. The court further recognized the difficulties for an individual to prove that a large industry was negligent. It, therefore, decided to abandon the onus of proving there were both a buyer and seller and of finding fault and, instead, held responsible the individual or corporation in the best position to pay.

To people concerned with the economics of injury, these decisions made a great deal of sense. The industry will be expected to insure against losses caused by defective products, the loss will be spread among those who are a part of that industry, rather than the entire burden falling on one manufacturer, and the cost will again be spread among a wide group of consumers who use that product. As the pay-off to the victim, the people injured by the industry will be compensated and, in this way, justice will be served. The time is near when we will simply ask whether or not the individual was injured as a result of using a particular product, regardless of fault.

No-fault reform brought distinct economic benefits to those

injured as a result of product accidents. Despite a no-fault
approach, the individual recovers the full extent of his economic loss, medical costs, pain and suffering including mental anguish, and whatever other unique, general, or intangible damages caused by the incident. The theory of strict
liability, so often cited by proponents of no-fault insurance,
has resulted in the abandonment of negligence as a standard
for assessing liability; nevertheless, in many situations, it
provides full payment to the injured. Even in the case of
workmen's compensation, where recovery was hard to obtain at common law, the damages awarded are far more
liberal than would be available under virtually all no-fault
automobile insurance plans.

Change in the law of negligence demonstrates the flexibility of our legal tradition. With shifting social goals, the
system was remarkable in its ability to bend with the times
and was easily adapted to the automobile. In the early
part of the twentieth century, an inevitable flood of accidents accompanied the upsurge in the number of cars. The
law of negligence emphasizing fault had reached a crest,
and the motorist fitted in neatly. The doctrine of the reasonable man, for example, could easily be applied to what the
reasonable man who was operating an automobile would
prudently do in a similar situation.

The fault system also acted as a deterrent against careless driving, but in a different way than is commonly supposed. Bad drivers are not deterred from bad driving by the
possibility of a lawsuit, but fault-finding acts as a deterrent
because the careless driver knows that he will not recover
his own losses if he causes accidents and that he will be
forced to shoulder his own expenses. As a question of social
policy, is it wise to eliminate this deterrent effect from accident law?

The law of torts provides victims of accidents the oppor-

tunity to be compensated for their damages. Regardless of
whether recovery is offered on the basis of strict liability or
fault, the object has always been to compensate adequately
the innocent victim. The negligence system worked well
while automobiles were possessed by relatively few. But,
with an increase in traffic, deficiencies were exposed, particularly the fact that some worthy victims were unable to collect for their injuries. The most serious difficulty in accident
cases was not proving someone was negligent or at fault. Because 40 per cent of traffic accidents are rear-end collisions
and a large percentage of accidents involve drivers who are
flagrantly violating the law—drunk drivers, speeders, stop-
sign runners—it is not difficult to place blame. The problem
was that most defendants could not pay.

With the growth of casualty insurance, liability coverage
was offered to protect automobile owners from lawsuits and
to guard against personal assets' being carted away by a successful plaintiff. The device of insurance was initially designed to protect the wrongdoer rather than compensate the
injured. Since many drivers failed to carry liability insurance, successful litigants often went unpaid because of the
impossibility of obtaining funds from an insolvent defendant. To combat this injustice, Massachusetts in 1927 became the first state to compel the purchase of automobile
liability insurance. For the first time, a state tied permission
to operate a car on the public highway to the possession of
automobile insurance. New York and North Carolina followed, but not until late in the 1950's.

While Massachusetts went in the direction of compulsory
insurance, the rest of the country passed legislation calling
for "financial responsibility." A car could be driven on the
highway of a state with a financial responsibility law without insurance of any kind. A driver who was involved in an
accident caused by his own negligence was required to

show that he was financially capable of paying for the damages. If he could prove he was insured or that he had independent funds to pay for his victim's expenses, he was allowed to continue driving. But, if the wrongdoer was financially irresponsible—no insurance, no assets—he lost the right to drive, pending the payment of any lawsuit judgment against him.

Commonly, those states that had financial responsibility laws formed uninsured-motorist pools, financed by a surcharge on automobile registration and used to cover unpaid claims. This type of insurance arrangement still works well in less populated areas, but, in the more industrial and urban states, financial responsibility has run aground. Because of the increase in accident frequency, accompanied by a rapid rise in the cost of claims, the uninsured motorist pools dry up rapidly. The weakness is that everyone gets one free accident—one bite of the apple—before being called upon to purchase liability insurance. Because all drivers pay money into the pool, the cost of the first accident is absorbed by society rather than by the careless individual or a private insurance company.

The introduction of compulsory automobile insurance, as well as financial responsibility, did nothing to change the law of negligence. What had changed was the purpose of insurance. The state now demanded insurance coverage from drivers to protect the innocent traffic victim, instead of shielding a careless defendant from being successfully sued. Both provide that a driver offer minimum security to those he might injure on the road. But, with the runaway volume of traffic accidents, the trend of disaffection with compulsory insurance and financial responsibility as effective means of coping with rising insurance costs and efficiently spreading benefits has increased. Cost efficiency is the new watchword.

Reparation plans of today have within them large measures of waste, scattering resources in many directions other than back to the victim. Reform is on its way, but confining the issue to a choice of fault or no-fault is insufficient. Accident law must be updated to encourage accident prevention, administrative efficiency, equitable benefit-spreading at a reasonable cost, and the coordination of all social and private insurance schemes.

But this must not be achieved at the price of elevating the role of insurance to a level higher than the law it is supposed to serve. Insurance should remain supplementary to compensating victims and spreading accident risks. Now we are experiencing attempts by the industry to rewrite the law to bring it into harmony with its own purposes. As a matter of economics, in order to make more people eligible to be compensated under the no-fault system, benefits to the innocent have been reduced to a skeleton of what they were under the common-law system. In the quest for the best possible system of insurance, we must find the right mixture of fault and no-fault principles, without sacrificing the legacy of fairness that has characterized our system of law.

The law must not exist for the benefit of the insurance industry. The foremost goal of reform must be providing compensation to accident victims fairly and completely at a cost society can afford. Before it is too late, we must ask: Are we on the right road?

3

The Boston Massacre

ON JANUARY 1, 1971, the nation's first no-fault automobile insurance bill went into effect in Massachusetts. On route to
its enactment this legislation was the subject of one of the
fiercest, most prolonged and confused legislative battles in
the tumultuous history of Massachusetts politics, involving
the insurance industry, the two major political parties, the
State Legislature, labor and consumer groups, the bar, and
the automobile insurance reformers in a four-year whirlpool
of activity and counteractivity. The Massachusetts experience is the prototype of what can be expected to recur
throughout the country.

Massachusetts was an appropriate place for a first attempt
at automobile insurance reform. Because of high personal injury claim frequency and high average payments per claim,
the state has been plagued for years with expensive automobile coverage. Opinions differ as to why this was the case,
but it is assumed that the costs of Massachusetts automobile
insurance escalated due to obvious physical deficiencies.

Road systems are poorly designed, dangerous, and in many
cases obsolete. Unpredictable New England weather conditions make driving treacherous on the best of highways.
Massachusetts daily generates massive volumes of traffic, especially during winter, when most commuting takes place
in darkness. Superimposed upon unusually unsafe driving
conditions is the insistence of Detroit to produce overpowered and uncrashworthy automobiles unsuited to protect occupants from the dangers caused by collisions even
at low speeds. High insurance rates were also in part due to
spotty law enforcement. The percentage of Massachusetts
drivers convicted of moving traffic violations remained the
lowest in the country. The Massachusetts conviction rate
was one-sixth that of the Pacific coast states for correspond-
ing years during the late 1960's.

Aside from factors incidentally related to insurance, the
system of compulsory insurance that existed in Massachusetts since 1927 encouraged personal injury claims. Massachusetts' compulsory insurance liability law was never accompanied by a compulsory property damage law. This
meant that property damage claims were frequently submitted disguised as personal injury claims to protect against
the possible absence of coverage to pay the repair bill for a
damaged automobile. This practice was so common that,
when insurance reform was first being considered, the phe-
nomenon of property damage claims filed as personal injury
claims was acknowledged as a significant rating factor by
every report on Bay State insurance. Because of the rewards
and low personal risk of filing such fictitious claims, this cus-
tom overlapped into cases that were absolutely fraudulent.

But the principal element in the unusually high cost of
automobile insurance in Massachusetts was a statute that
handed to the commissioner of insurance the power to set
rates as long as he deemed them just, reasonable, adequate,

and nondiscriminatory. Uniform rate-setting resulted in the elimination of any market-place competition among the insurers. By law, no insurance company was permitted to sell compulsory automobile insurance at rates below those set by the commissioner. This discouraged some of the better managed companies from operating in Massachusetts.

The system was also frustrating and slow. In some counties it took three or four years to receive a jury trial. Nor did the companies do anything to expedite claim payment by efficient handling, complaining instead about the sheer volume. By the late 1960's, it was apparent that a drastic overhaul of automobile insurance was needed. It was from this starting point that no-fault automobile insurance began its journey from abstract principle to political reality.

It began when the Keeton-O'Connell plan came to the attention of Representative Michael Dukakis, who happened to be a former student of Robert Keeton at Harvard Law School. Dukakis arranged a meeting with Keeton to discuss the plan; and the movement for the passage of Massachusetts no-fault was under way. Within weeks, it was filed by Dukakis in the Massachusetts Legislature and being considered by a joint legislative committee on automobile insurance. In spite of the fact that the committee recommended against it, in August, 1967, the Keeton-O'Connell plan was brought to the floor of the Massachusetts House of Representatives, the lower branch of the Massachusetts Legislature, for a vote. To the surprise of everyone, including Dukakis, the bill was passed by the House and sent to the Massachusetts Senate for concurrence. Panic set in, and the insurance industry and the bar, acting in concert, exerted their influence on the Senate, urging it to defeat the plan.

Up to then, there had been little public debate on the bill's merits and minimal understanding of what it was all about. The favorable vote by the House was a symptom of a more serious disease. Sentiment for reform was sufficiently strong that the Legislature grabbed the first attractive proposal to come along. The insurance industry was so taken by surprise that it had not as yet adopted a policy stand on no-fault other than to express lame interest and to request an opportunity to make financial predictions and thereby discover more about the price features of the new insurance. The insurance industry in Massachusetts had been saddled with what it considered were inadequate rates for compulsory personal injury coverage and was interested in any reform that would offer greater profits on compulsory coverage.

John A. Volpe, then Governor of Massachusetts and later Secretary of the Department of Transportation in the Nixon Administration, indicated that, if the Massachusetts Senate were to pass the Keeton-O'Connell bill, he would veto it. In the weeks that elapsed between the House passage and Senate vote, there was feverish political activity. For weeks, the subject captured the news. Newspapers editorialized and the television stations donated public time for debates between the proponents and opponents of the plan. When the Massachusetts Senate eventually acted, it defeated the plan by a three-to-one margin. Keeton-O'Connell was then returned to the House, which on a second vote reversed its earlier position and killed the plan. Although it was clear the Legislature was itching to do something, no insurance reform emerged from the 1967 session. Since reform was a politically popular issue and a sure way to draw votes, the search for possible alternatives to Massachusetts compulsory insurance began in earnest.

The passage of the plan in the House marked the high-water mark for Keeton-O'Connell; this was as close as it would ever come to being passed by a legislature. In addition to postponing action to gain time for further study of the issues, the Legislature, using its power to regulate insurance, imposed a freeze on any increases of compulsory automobile insurance rates. This meant that the price of liability insurance for personal injury coverage was not going to be increased until a solution was agreed upon. The freeze was designed to give the insurers added incentive to come up with an acceptable plan for reform.

During 1968 and 1969, the insurance industry, caught off guard by the near passage of Keeton-O'Connell, began to think seriously about applying no-fault to their own purposes. The industry is divided into three major groups of companies—stock, mutual, and independent companies. The stock companies are owned by shareholders in the same way that a corporation is held. The mutuals are owned by the policyholders and do not issue stock. The independents are a mixture of stock and mutual companies which choose not to affiliate with either group.

The stock companies' trade organization, the American Insurance Association, led by its president, T. Lawrence Jones, decided to give its firm support to no-fault insurance. The American Insurance Association's position was even more extreme in the direction of no-fault than the Keeton-O'Connell plan. No-fault looked like a money-maker beyond the AIA's wildest dreams: It was compulsory insurance with low overhead and high investment return potential. The mutuals, because they sell insurance directly without using agents, were more satisfied with the established system than were the stock companies. They sell the same product as the stock companies, and at the same price, but with lower marketing costs. And since they are policyholder-oriented, they tend to be more concerned about the quality of the service. The mutual companies were not as eager to go along with no-fault as their stock company brethren. They took a wait-and-see attitude, and eventually supported a partial no-fault plan operating in harmony with a revised fault system.

In April, 1968, a special insurance commission was set up by the Legislature to study the entire automobile insurance question to arrive at recommendations for change. It was composed of thirteen members: three were members of the State Senate and were appointed by the president of the Senate, five were members of the State House of Representatives and were appointed by the speaker of the House, five were at-large members and were appointed by the governor. This was a last attempt to bring representatives from all factions together for the purpose of grinding out a solution acceptable to all concerned.

Among those included on this special commission, in addition to the legislators, was David Lane, who represented the independent brokers and agents and who ultimately filed the bill that would become law. The commissioner of insurance, Eugene Farnum, was appointed, as was the vice-president of Employers Commercial Union Insurance Company, Ian Heap, who was there to represent the stock companies' interest. Richard Schannon, general counsel of American Mutual Insurance Company, was named to represent the mutuals. The President of the Massachusetts chapter of the American Trial Lawyers, Thomas Cargill, joined the committee as the trial bar's representative. The commission held twenty public hearings and issued its recommendations for insurance reform in January, 1970. Of the thirteen members, only eight signed the majority report, while the remaining five members filed separate dissenting opinions. The battle lines were drawn.

The majority came forward with a plan that it identified as the "safe-driver plan." Instead of being a plan at all, it was actually a set of six diverse proposals for insurance revision and highway safety. It was heralded as an attempt to eliminate the financial problems tied to Massachusetts automobile insurance by introducing financial responsibility, joined to a merit rating proposal designed to reduce costs for accident-free drivers. The report called for the adoption of a package of loosely related bills that it hoped would provide added highway safety, cost reduction in insurance, relief of court congestion, and a more honest approach toward the filing of damage claims.

Of the six proposals, only two could fairly be described as significant insurance reforms. The first of the two called for the enactment of no-fault property damage. Drivers would be given the choice of insuring their cars with their own insurance company by purchasing a collision policy or, as an alternative, relinquishing their right to sue for property damage based on proving fault. The objective was to reduce total insurance costs by eliminating the need to purchase property damage insurance. The property damage reform provided that payments had to be made by the insurer within fifteen days after filing a claim. The commissioner of insurance would be charged with taking actions—unspecified in the report—against companies that took longer.

The second proposal relating to insurance was the offer of an optional $250 deductible to help the costs of compulsory personal injury coverage. A deductible is a cost-saving device by which a policyholder agrees to pay the first portion of a claim out of his own funds in order to hold down the price of his insurance. By choosing a deductible, the insured whose negligence was established as the cause of an injury would be responsible to his victim out of his own pocket for the first $250. The idea was to involve those who cause accidents in the payment process, and to set up a deterrent by involving the careless party directly. The purchase of a $250 deductible would decrease the cost of a liability policy, although self-insuring can hardly be called a saving.

The other four reform proposals bore only an incidental

relationship to automobile insurance. The commission suggested that reports of attending doctors and estimates from automobile repair shops be signed and submitted to the companies under the pains and penalties of perjury. It recommended a vehicle title act to protect the motoring public from automobile thefts, which were encouraged by the confusion of tracing automobile ownership. The third proposal was to broaden the scope of the Fraudulent Claims Bureau to enable it to investigate all kinds of accident claims. Finally, the commission landed upon a highway safety program—a catch-all that included such diverse items as schoolbus control and retread tire standards. While the last four recommendations were meaningful, they scarcely qualify as major insurance reform.

The five separate minority reports that were filed, each reflecting the attitudes of the major interests, were evidence of the lack of agreement over the future of automobile insurance reform. By now, the players had firmed up their strategy for change. Representative Dukakis, who had originally introduced Keeton-O'Connell, was particularly hard on the majority report. In his dissenting opinion, he wrote that, with the exception of the liability deduction option and no-fault property damage, the list did nothing to solve automobile insurance problems in Massachusetts. He rejected the majority's belief that the culprit in automobile insurance was the citizen and not the system itself. Dukakis again urged passage of the Keeton-O'Connell Plan.

Senator William Randall, the lone Republican senator on the committee, reflected his party's attitude. He was not ideologically opposed to no-fault but he was concerned that the Keeton-O'Connell plan might be too harsh in denying pain-and-suffering benefits in the more serious cases. He was prepared to compromise.

The stock companies, through Ian Heap of Employers-

Commercial Union, recommended total no-fault, as promoted by the American Insurance Association. An AIA total no-fault plan eliminates the right of an accident victim, under any circumstances, to obtain general damages, including pain and suffering, regardless of the severity of his injury. Heap dismissed the majority report, saying it failed to advance any effective solutions to present automobile insurance deficiencies.

The fourth report, reflecting the attitudes of the mutual companies, was submitted by Richard Schannon, general counsel for the American Mutual Insurance Company. Of all the minority reports, Schannon's comes closest to reaching a middle ground between the competing factions which, on the one hand, sought to impose total or near-total no-fault, while, on the other, trying to retain the fault system with only incidental changes. Schannon departed from the other minority reports because he agreed with the majority that a total or near total no-fault insurance bill was not the optimum solution. The only possibility for reducing the cost of insurance, other than accident prevention, would be to reduce benefits paid to victims. He argued lower premiums meant fewer benefits—that is no mystery—and anticipated that the public would be shocked and outraged when it realized how little it was going to receive from the more radical no-fault plans, including Keeton-O'Connell and the AIA. Schannon pointed to the conveniently ignored statistics that the cost of personal injury insurance under the fault system had not risen nearly as rapidly in recent years as had income levels and medical expenses.

Rather than adopt a total no-fault system, Schannon suggested a series of less spectacular reforms for improving negligence laws. He stressed the importance of removing the need for the insurance companies to dispose of small and doubtful claims in order to control their administrative costs.

The cure offered by Schannon on behalf of the mutuals was an effort to satisfy both the fault and no-fault camps. The mutuals wanted two key reforms. First, they were interested in applying objective standards to measure intangible general damages by linking them to the amount of the medical bill—payment for pain and suffering could not exceed the medical bill. Secondly, they wanted economic losses to be paid, regardless of fault, for the small claim.

The final minority report, filed by David Lane, representing the agents and brokers, was extremely critical of the majority opinion. Lane found it incredible that, while the country was demanding expanded motoring protection, the Massachusetts commission was seeking to impose deductibles and the elimination of the guarantee that insurance funds would be available to all traffic accident victims. To overlay a series of deductibles on a liability system would only invite padding of claims, increased litigation, and public dissatisfaction.

He also made a pitch for free competition among insurance companies in order to provide safe drivers with better rates and to bring about intelligent merit-rating to spread insurance costs equitably. He argued that because Massachusetts insurance rates are set up by the commissioner of insurance, the lack of open competition hurt the agents. He pointed to the direct writers, particularly the mutuals, who do not use insurance agents and therefore do not pay commissions, and who are able to write fixed-rate insurance more economically. With losses from compulsory insurance rising yearly, the agents had seen their commissions cut back by the companies. In a burst of enlightened self-interest, the agents and brokers lent their support to the "personal injury protection" bill. This proposal became the plan around which the insurers eventually rallied as the unspoken compromise between the stock and mutual companies and the plan that finally passed the Legislature and was signed into law.

Since the battle was based on ideology and philosophy, neither side was willing to concede anything of much substance. The fight to install no-fault was to be bitter and uncompromising. Although the no-fault advocates were eventually able to agree on a plan among themselves, they were incapable of getting together with those favoring the retention of the fault system to work out an agreement. The dissolution of the special insurance commission in February, 1970, was the last straw to grasp in the search for a suitable compromise before the subject of automobile insurance became engulfed in the political hysteria that followed.

On the surface, the study commission looked like a lost opportunity for the advocates of a better fault system to convince its critics that there were acceptable alternatives to Massachusetts compulsory insurance, without throwing away most of the law of negligence. Regardless of how brilliant the suggestions for fault reform, it was unlikely that the no-fault supporters were going to change their minds, foreseeing the financial bonanza that was coming to the insurance companies once no-fault was passed. And by failing to devise a suitable alternative to no-fault, it was considerably easier for uncommitted legislators to grab the no-fault banner. They had no other standard. By early 1970, it was apparent to even the most shortsighted that some kind of no-fault legislation was rapidly approaching.

Hovering over the forces having a direct stake in automobile insurance reform were the political parties. The Republicans had in the past supported legislation that would replace Massachusetts compulsory insurance with a financial responsibility law. After John Volpe resigned as governor to accept the cabinet post as DOT Secretary, the Republican Party shifted its position. His replacement, Fran-

cis Sargent, after months of noncommitment, finally endorsed a limited no-fault concept. At the state Republican
convention held in the spring of 1970, the Republicans un-
qualifiedly supported a no-fault platform. It was an election
year, and, because of a state constitutional change, the gov-
ernorship of Massachusetts was, for the first time, lengthened from a two-year to a four-year term. The issue of
insurance reform, in the news constantly since 1967, became
the principal campaign issue. By now, no-fault insurance
was enjoying the enthusiastic endorsement of the news media, particularly the powerful *Boston Globe* and the local
radio and television stations. Together, they editorialized
in favor of the adoption of a no-fault plan, heralding cost
savings for the consumer.

The Democrats, as is customary in Massachusetts, were
hopelessly split. The Democratic nominee for governor,
Maurice Donahue, was serving as President of the Massachusetts Senate. The Democratic convention had endorsed
a plank promising a limited no-fault reform, which was a
Morse Code method of saying that the party had not as yet
agreed to support no-fault wholeheartedly. In 1967, Donahue had been one of the most influential senators in defeat-
ing Keeton-O'Connell after it had passed the House. In his
bid to become governor, his running mate for lieutenant
governor was none other than Michael Dukakis, the most ardent no-fault champion in the Legislature. The House of
Representatives, which was overwhelmingly Democratic and
strongly influenced by Dukakis, was extremely receptive to
passing some form of no-fault. The Senate, on the other
hand, was committed to the retention of a revitalized fault
system. When the Massachusetts Legislature convened in
1970, it was confronted by approximately 350 bills dealing
with insurance reform.

Compounding the confusion and acrimony that would ordinarily be expected to accompany such a dramatic change-over was the political maneuvering that influenced the debate that followed. There was a general consensus on the need to rearrange the entire insurance system, and it was a foregone conclusion that compulsory liability coverage would not survive the session. But with the wide assortment of proposals and counterproposals to choose from, little opportunity remained to evaluate the competing merits of the many plans proposed.

The insurance industry interests finally agreed to end their intramural impasse and threw their combined support behind the brokers' and agents' "personal injury protection" plan, a consensus between the stock and mutual companies, who had been at loggerheads over which plan they could together support. The brokers' and agents' bill was characterized as a compromise no-fault bill, but it was a compromise only in so far as it provided a rallying point for the two most powerful factions within the insurance industry. Because the industry realized that it could not overtly sponsor an insurance bill and expect to gather enough public support for its passage, it made good sense to line up behind the brokers' and agents' bill. The companies did not delude themselves into thinking that they were sufficiently popular to have a plan sponsored directly by them passed by the Legislature.

"Personal injury protection" received the belated support of Dukakis, who doggedly stayed with Keeton-O'Connell until he realized that a bill so restrictive was not going to be acceptable. Governor Sargent bestowed his blessing on the brokers' and agents' plan. The Massachusetts Consumer's Council also announced its support. As the clincher, the news media, the *Boston Globe* in the vanguard, insisted the Legislature pass this bill immediately.

"Personal injury protection" began its triumphant march

through the Legislature by receiving a favorable report from the joint legislative committee on insurance. By now, the only opponents left to contend with were the trial lawyers, who steadfastly held out against the plan. Their efforts to defeat no-fault were doomed to futility. They failed to come forward with a viable alternative proposal, and no matter how sound their objections, they were cast aside as mere gut responses motivated by financial self-interest.

As the options narrowed, only two courses of action were open: Pass the brokers' and agents' bill or stay with compulsory insurance. "Personal injury protection" was first considered by the Senate ways and means committee. The committee chairman, Senator James Burke, thereupon referred the bill to a subcommittee consisting of three members, which reported it back favorably. It was agreed that, if the bill could win passage by the Massachusetts Senate, the House of Representatives would go along. With Sargent publicly supporting the bill and announcing that he would submit no plan of his own, there was no doubt that he would sign. When the floor fight began in the Senate, it was recognized that this would be the widest river to cross before Massachusetts could enact no-fault.

As soon as the debate began, a parliamentary move was made to substitute the retention of compulsory insurance reinforced by a companion merit-rating proposal recommended by the special insurance commission, in place of the brokers' and agents' bill. The Senate accepted the substitute proposal and, by a comfortable margin, passed the compulsory insurance–merit-rating system. But this victory for the fault advocates was short-lived.

When the substitute bill was transmitted to the House of Representatives for concurrence, a second substitution took place. This time, the House elected to install its own version of "personal injury protection," but attached an important rider that guaranteed a 15 per cent across-the-board price reduction applicable to every form of automobile insurance. The reduction was not restricted to personal injury coverage but was also applied to property damage, fire and theft, collision, medical payments, and protection against uninsured motorists. Sporadic efforts to sidetrack the bill met with no success, and the bill was voted through by a margin of about four-to-one. The political hot potato was tossed back to the Senate. The promise of a 15 per cent across-the-board reduction in the total cost of automobile insurance made what was once popular now irresistible. The impression that a cut was possible was fostered despite the knowledge that such a reduction was wholly illegal. The prospect of unconstitutionality did not slow down the proponents, who proceeded to announce savings running into millions, and all at the expense of the insurance companies. What voter could help but admire a candidate making this offer?

When no-fault returned to the Senate, a second series of parliamentary maneuvers took place. The Democrats unveiled several plans that had not been previously considered by any of the various committees on insurance. As a last resort, the old financial responsibility plan promoted in 1967 by Governor Volpe was dragged out of mothballs and dusted off. Financial responsibility had been routinely filed by the Republicans since 1967. When it was brought to the Senate floor, it caused a considerable amount of Republican embarrassment, because Republican senators were caught in the position of having to oppose a bill they once so strongly favored and had themselves filed. The financial responsibility bill, with a merit-rating system attached, looked to be destined for passage by the Senate, unless another strategy switch took place. Had the financial responsibility act been approved, it was unlikely that the House would have gone along. If it did not, a compromise committee would have been formed and no insurance bill would have been enacted during the 1970 session.

With an election in the balance, that possibility was unthinkable to both parties, who were eager to take credit for reform. The Senate, in a bewildering third substitution, now returned to the no-fault brokers' and agents' bill it had earlier rejected and passed it. The no-fault opponents had come to realize that nothing but no-fault was going to pass. The voted bill contained two important new amendments. First, insurance policies were made noncancelable except for nonpayment, conviction of driving under the influence of liquor or drugs, and fraud. Second, the 15 per cent across-the-board reduction on all lines of insurance was again tacked on.

The insurance companies suddenly soured in their support of the bill. They were faced with the distasteful possibility of reducing the price of insurance and eliminating the right to cancel. To the companies, this was almost un-American. The Senate had legislated the reduction that the no-fault proponents had advertised. From the Senate, the bill returned once again to the House, where it was quickly approved, but only after a further amendment was added, making all other parts of the bill constitutional even if one portion was declared unconstitutional. The two Senate amendments were left alone.

The strategy of the Democrats and the no-fault opponents was based on the assumption that Governor Sargent would be unable to sign the bill as passed, because of insurance industry opposition. The gubernatorial election was only three months away, and there were political issues involved that transcended automobile insurance reform. The Democratic-controlled Legislature hoped that the Governor would be backed into a corner, faced with having to veto a bill that he had openly advocated. The Democrats could then charge that Sargent was the insincere lackey of the insurance industry and that he had blocked the last chance for insurance reform as soon as the companies told him to.

On the day that the Legislature gave its final approval, four of the biggest insurance companies—Travelers Insurance Companies, Aetna Life and Casualty, Lumbermens Mutual Casualty Company, and the Employers-Commercial Union —which wrote about 30 per cent of the automobile insurance in Massachusetts, announced that they were withdrawing from the state and would no longer be issuing policies after January 1, 1971. Employers-Commercial Union, which had been constructing a multistory office building in downtown Boston, ceased construction and announced that it was moving operations to New Hampshire. It was expected that the entire automobile insurance industry would threaten to follow suit.

Sargent had several options. He could sign the bill as presented to him by the Legislature, but, by signing, he would risk having the insurance companies walk out. This would have resulted in chaos, if 2,600,000 motorists were unable to insure their automobiles as of January. Sargent could choose to veto, but, by taking this course, he would leave himself open to the charge that he blocked insurance reform, and he would have appeared to be opposed to the illegal 15 per cent rate reduction, which for a master politician was beyond consideration in an election year. As a final option, he could sign the bill and resubmit it to the Legislature, which was still in session, for emergency repairs.

When the insurers threatened to leave the state, because of their displeasure with the 15 per cent across-the-board rate reduction and the noncancelability clause, their attitude toward no-fault was misinterpreted by the public. At no time did the industry object to the passage of a no-fault bill. On the contrary, the insurance industry, having done its homework in anticipating future profits, had promoted no-fault with the Legislature. But by the threat to leave, the misconception arose that the underlying reason was the industry's fear of no-fault. Because most of the public believed that the insurance industry was opposed to it, no-fault reform became more popular than ever.

Further confusing the passage of no-fault was the strange behavior of the brokers and agents. Immediately following the announcement by the insurers that they were pulling out, the agents organized a protest march on the State House, to urge Sargent not to sign the very bill that their organization had sponsored. Once faced with the prospect of the companies' leaving, the agents were concerned with their own welfare. Massachusetts Attorney General Robert Quinn went on the offensive against the insurers by ordering an investigation into alleged antitrust violations arising from the synchronized action of the insurance companies in taking steps to influence this legislature to their own advantage. After the threat of investigation, the insurers maintained silence but quietly made preparation to leave.

It was within this surrealistic atmosphere that, on the evening of Thursday, August 13, 1970, Sargent faced the television cameras and, with a straight face and grand flourish, signed the country's first no-fault insurance bill into law. What an opportunity for a gubernatorial candidate! He intoned that he would not succumb to the threats made by the insurance industry and that no amount of coercion would keep him from signing the bill. Having appeared to criticize the insurance industry, he turned to the Legislature, saying that he "would keep the Legislature in session until hell freezes over" if it failed to delete the objectionable amendments. He then proposed emergency legislation to eliminate the insurance company reservations about the bill. Although it was tacitly understood that the 15 per cent across-the-board reduction was invalid, Governor Sargent did not dare tackle this. No candidate for governor could be expected to deprive the electorate of a proposed 15 per cent saving in insurance costs three months prior to an election.

After the passage and signing, the public anxiously awaited the outcome of the insurance industry's action. Some companies notified their employees that they would no longer be needed after the end of the year. The state attempted to meet this emergency by preparing to establish a state-run insurance pool, eliminating the need for insurance companies; estimates that a state-run pool would require $500 million in initial funding put a chill on this alternative.

As an aftermath of the Governor's speech, the Legislature passed two reform amendments. It agreed to eliminate the noncancelability protection. The insurers again gained power to cancel for all the usual excuses, excluding old age and extreme youth. In reality, the insurers could issue policies in the old arbitrary way. Nothing had changed. This solved half the problem of the insurance companies. Because no one dared to take on the elimination of the 15 per cent across-the-board reduction, the companies were forced to turn to the courts to recover this amount.

During the time between the filing of suit and the Massachusetts Supreme Court's decision, additional companies joined the walkout. Speculation was that 40 per cent of the insurance written in 1970 was not going to be renewed. Still awaiting the Supreme Court decision, on November 3, 1970, Governor Sargent was re-elected governor for a full four-year term. A week later, the Massachusetts Supreme Court ruled that the 15 per cent reduction applied to all lines of automobile insurance was unconstitutional. The companies announced their intention to remain and, to prove it, increased the cost of property damage by 38.4 per cent for 1971. Sargent and the insurers had won.

4
Massachusetts No-Fault

THE VERSION OF NO-FAULT AUTOMOBILE INSURANCE adopted by the Massachusetts Legislature satisfied none of the participants in the no-fault fight—except the insurance industry. In the Legislature's haste to get the insurance issue off dead center, it passed a mixed bag of compromises designed to satisfy the consumer, the politicans, the insurance industry, the insurance agents, and particularly the press. As one member put it, "This legislature is going to pass something even if it's a laundry bill."

Massachusetts left within its plan a method of keeping alive at least some of the traditional possibilities for recovery and retained the concept of fault for a limited number of cases. Pain and suffering—or general damage claims, as they are called—are still allowed within unevenly drawn exceptions, limited to rare situations in which the victim, after first proving fault, could show that his injury falls within one of six categories. A general-damage claim, in addition to economic loss, can be compensated in the following situations: where the medical bill exceeds $500; where a permanent and serious disfigurement results; where there is a loss, totally or partially, of vision or hearing as defined by the Massachusetts Workmen's Compensation Act; where there is a loss totally or partially of a bodily member; where the injury results in fracture; where the injury results in death. Inclusion within one of these categories permits an accident victim to retain his common-law right to a suit for general damages.

Professor Jeffrey O'Connell, the co-author of the original no-fault basic protection plan, said he was disappointed that the thresholds for fault claims were left so low that the possibility of a claim for pain and suffering by inclusion under one of these exceptions was kept alive. He felt that the $500 mark for allowing a general damage claim made it tempting to pad a medical bill. As a practical matter, these thresholds will eliminate at least 95 per cent of all negligence claims for personal injuries. The $500 plateau in the overwhelming number of claims can be reached after in-patient hospitalization for a minimum of two or three days followed by post-hospital treatment by a private physician. The effect of this statute is to bar all but a small percentage of people involved as accident victims from tort recovery for general damages. The remaining 5 per cent who are still eligible for full recovery have the added burden of having to prove that their accident was caused by someone else's carelessness. A fair estimate is that about 3 per cent of all those injured in automobile accidents will be able to make effective claims for compensation for general damages under Massachusetts no-fault.

The insurance agents who originally sponsored this no-fault bill—referred to previously as the brokers' and agents' bill—looked upon this type of reform as a method by which their special interests in the automobile insurance business could be saved. The companies had protested that they were losing money on automobile insurance in Massachusetts during the 1960's. As losses increased, commissions on compulsory insurance were cut. The agents looked upon no-fault as a way to revive commissions. Since the new coverage was compulsory, the agent fares no better under no-fault than he did with the fault system. High commissions are impossible when an artificial demand is created by making insurance compulsory, thus reducing the role of the agent to order-taking. No sales effort is needed to sell a product to a captive market. And with direct writing, neighborhood agents may have put themselves out of business.

With the growing practice of group sales in the field of casualty insurance, the insurance companies will sell directly to large blocks of drivers within a corporation or any other large group, deducting the cost of automobile insurance premiums from payrolls. No-fault insurance, especially in the way it can rate a risk for its own economic loss potential rather than predicting harm caused to others, lends itself to conversion to group insurance sales. The opportunity for modernizing market techniques, which by-pass the agencies, are boundless. The health-and-accident writers—giants such as Prudential, Metropolitan Life, John Hancock, and others —can be expected to convert their experience in this field and enter automobile casualty, because no-fault as legislated in Massachusetts is little more than a glorified health-and-accident insurance program. These carriers, because of their enormous financial strength, may well pre-empt the field.

Another group within the industry caught in the squeeze of the switch to a new form of coverage are the insurance employees. Insurance claim personnel, particularly adjusters and their back-up staffs, have been cut back. Automobile accidents, formerly handled on a field staff basis, are now being handled nearly exclusively by mail or by telephone and by a reduced staff of investigatory personnel, at a far cheaper cost to the companies. Moreover, efforts of management to block unionization of insurance employees has made it easy for it to eliminate jobs.

The trial bar was displeased with the passage of the no-fault bill for its own set of reasons. Instinctively, the organized bar resisted no-fault insurance from the very beginning. Because this resistance was so absolute and uncompromising, it lost an opportunity to help guide the immediate future of automobile insurance reform. The long-established political tactic of "pre-empting the center"—the rush to find a consensus—never happened in the no-fault fight. The trial bar would have been more successful in preserving the rights it sought to defend had it been more positive in its attitude toward some of the better features of no-fault. It was discouraging to see the disrepute in which the bar was held by the general public, the media, and the Legislature and disheartening to witness the futility of its disorganized and sporadic efforts to defeat a plan that it felt was unwise and unjust. The trial lawyers never managed to convince the public that its motives for opposing no-fault were not just based on self-interest, and its opponents effectively exploited this failure.

The consumer, who was the ostensible beneficiary of the plan, also had little reason to rejoice. The man on the street was told he could expect a reduction of 15 per cent on his total 1971 insurance bill. But the built-in 15 per cent no-fault cut ultimately applied only to compulsory personal injury coverage. The other companion automobile coverages, such as property damage and collision insurance, were later increased by as much as 38.4 per cent. The consumer, led to believe that his automobile insurance costs would decline, was hit with a net increase. Performance fell short of expectations. Though no-fault compulsory personal injury coverage went down, over-all insurance costs went up.

Craig Spangenburg, chairman of the American Trial Lawyers Auto Reparations Committee, likens the cost-benefit balance of no-fault to a child who buys a four-ounce chocolate bar for ten cents and then is told afterwards that he can buy a cheaper one-ounce bar for a nickel. The ten-cent four-ounce chocolate bar is the cost-benefit ratio of insurance purchased under the fault system; the five-cent one-ounce bar is no-fault's cost-benefit ratio. It may cost less, but there is no real saving because the product is worth less.

Meager reductions had resulted in the public's giving away the right to be fairly and fully compensated for general damages in all but a token number of automobile accidents. The consumer was put in the position of subsidizing the poorer driver, because fault no longer played a significant role in allowing recovery. The chronic repeaters would become the ultimate beneficiaries of this system, leaving the vast number of drivers who are accident free to be placed in the position of spreading the risk for the careless.

Specifically, the Massachusetts no-fault law guarantees a payment of up to a maximum of $2,000 to satisfy all economic losses caused by personal injuries arising out of automobile accidents regardless of fault. The $2,000 no-fault maximum is a three-fold benefit:

- Reasonable medical expenses are paid in full.
- 75 per cent of actual wages lost are paid.
- Expenses incurred for hiring substitute help are paid in full.

The latter category is new and works in the following way:

A housewife is now allowed to hire a babysitter during the period of her disability. A homeowner is permitted to hire a house painter, if in fact he himself is unable to paint and would have done so had there been no accident. This is a totally new approach to compensating economic loss, and there is no experience by which to judge how this feature will work.

The three possibilities for recovery under no-fault—medical bills, 75 per cent of wages lost, and substitute help—can combine to reach a $2,000 limit. Any other economic damages in excess of $2,000, however severe, are not compensated by Massachusetts no-fault. Pain and suffering, disfigurement, emotional distress, loss of profits, and so forth are ignored regardless of fault unless one of the six exceptions allowing a common-law suit are present. Should the combination of medical expenses, wages, and substitute help exceed the $2,000 limit, the victim is forced to sue as he always did on a fault basis for recovery of his economic loss over and above $2,000.

Suppose a man's loss of wages and his medical expenses caused by an automobile accident amount to a total of $3,000. He receives $2,000 from his own insurance company without questions relative to fault. He must then sue whoever caused the accident to obtain his additional $1,000 economic loss. Unless he qualifies under one of the six threshold exceptions allowing general damages already mentioned, this is all he recovers.

With respect to the lost-wage provision, Massachusetts no-fault provides what is known in the language of insurance as "secondary coverage." This means that all wages or income received from other sources—for example, from a union wage-continuation plan or from the generosity of one's employer—must first be exhausted before a no-fault claim for loss of wages can be paid. If wages are paid from a collateral source, there can be no recovery for them under the no-fault system. This feature of the Massachusetts plan has been criticized, because it feeds upon sources outside the automobile insurance policy to assist in reducing the cost of automobile insurance, and results in hidden costs. Someone must absorb the financial loss.

The use of wage-continuation plans as collateral payments has been vigorously opposed by the labor unions. They feel that a labor union, negotiating a wage-continuation plan, does so at the expense of obtaining more money for its members. Now this hard-fought-for benefit is being preyed upon by the automobile insurance industry to mitigate its own obligations, for which it has accepted insurance premiums.

The initial version of the Keeton-O'Connell plan used private medical insurance as a primary source and automobile insurance as a secondary source of compensating accident victims for their medical expenses. Under that plan, private or social insurance benefits had first to be exhausted before the no-fault automobile coverage could be used. Because of the objections of the private health insurance companies, notably Blue Cross and Blue Shield, this provision of the Keeton-O'Connell plan was abandoned in the Massachusetts bill. Collateral medical insurance is no longer considered primary and no longer needs to be exhausted before a no-fault claim for medical expenses can be made.

Under the Massachusetts plan, no-fault coverage is given to the following: the insured, the owner of the automobile, members of the insured's household, authorized persons who are operating the insured's automobile, the insured's guests and guests of the authorized operator, pedestrians who are struck by the insured or while an authorized individual is driving his car. This last feature of the Massachusetts no-fault bill is revolutionary; pedestrians who are struck by an automobile are treated as having contractual rights with that automobile owner's insurance company. They become quasi-policyholders of the stranger's insurance company.

Several persons are excluded from coverage: A person who is eligible for workmen's compensation insurance at the time of his injury; a person who is injured as a result of his own intentional act; those driving under the influence of drugs or liquor; criminals who were committing a felony at the time of their injury; a driver who was deliberately trying to injure others at the time he himself was injured. The exclusions adopted by the Massachusetts Legislature, missing from the original Keeton-O'Connell bill, have been generally followed in all other no-fault plans.

Periodic payments are another new feature of the Massachusetts bill. Under the fault system, claims were settled or won in court on a one-payment lump-sum basis. Resources were unavailable to the victim at the time of his greatest need—immediately after the accident. Should payment be delayed for a number of years, as was often the case in catastrophic accidents, the victim faced financial hardship. The no-fault system closes this time gap by making periodic payments available during those periods when the victim, because of his incapacitation, is in greatest financial need. Unfortunately, the $2,000 no-fault limit can easily be exhausted in a month or two. Such a low no-fault benefit will do little for individuals forced to undergo extended periods of convalescence. Michael Dukakis, the leading proponent of no-fault, aptly described this low maximum saying, "The Massachusetts Legislature labored a year and brought forth a mouse."

Just as criticism of the tort reparation system was rightfully directed toward its tendency to overpay nuisance and medium-size claims, the same weakness is carried over to the no-fault system by the $2,000 limit. No-fault still pays an overabundance of small claims, which, by drawing on the total money available to compensate victims, freezes the $2,000 limit. If the public were to self-insure for the first $100 or $200 of economic loss, the pool from which to pay severely injured victims could be expanded. In this way, more money would be available to raise the maximum limit of $2,000 to a level that would do more for the seriously injured, without increasing the price of insurance. Keeton-O'Connell had such a device in the original plan, but Massachusetts chose to ignore it.

In an attempt to alleviate the hardships brought about by having to await a lump-sum payment, the insurance industry under the fault system has been experimenting with an advanced-payments plan that would allow payments to be credited to the company as a fund to be set off against any subsequent settlement. Several states are considering this type of advance payment along with their own insurance reform, which is far more sensible than discarding the entire tort system for the sake of periodic payments.

The relative costs of Massachusetts no-fault, the benefits, when a claim based on fault is still permitted, who is eligible and who is not, and when benefits are due are clear enough, but there are several trouble spots. In the liability section of the bill, a weak effort is made to use the cost-equity balance as a factor in making judgments as to which claims ought to be handled on a no-fault basis and which should continue under the tort system, but the results are often arbitrary and inconsistent. A suit for complete general damages based upon fault must fall within one of the six categories previously mentioned. The most commonly occurring of these categories will be the accumulation of $500 in medical bills—one of the six ways to open the door to a tort settlement. The effort to choose a dollar threshold as a fair balance of cost

and equity is misplaced. Any figure chosen—$500 or other-
wise—does not represent a rational basis for making a division of rights. It implies that the cost of one's medical services indicates the severity of an injury. Although in some
cases there may be a high correlation of medical cost to injury, it is not sufficiently universal to form the basis for a
rule to be used as the cut-off point for compensating all
cases.

Moreover, the $500 threshold is inherently discriminatory.
The odds are that an individual who, because of his social
and economic background, is used to the very best of medical services will reach this threshold far more frequently
than his poorer counterpart, who would ordinarily get his
medical services from a clinic or from a less expensive neighborhood physician. Nor does the Massachusetts statute answer whether or not individuals who receive free medical
assistance can ever qualify for the $500 medical threshold.
A person serving in the armed forces receiving treatment at
a military post is not presented with a bill; the law as it reads
says he is therefore not eligible for the $500 exception.

By all logical standards, the $500 threshold in Massa-
chusetts was chosen without any evidence that it was connected in any way to the general damages that an accident
victim suffers. Lower premiums was the only guideline.
What the actuaries did was to take a number at which no-
fault would be financially competitive with the price of
liability coverage, and assign it the status of a threshold. A
more accurate method of identifying the most equitable
cut-off would be to base that threshold upon a standard that
fits the injury involved. It is better to place the right to recover for general damages on the type and quality of medical attention, together with the length of convalescence
necessary to restore health, than resort to an arbitrary
medical-cost figure.

When the bill was put together, it was written under such pressure that it suffers from poor draftsmanship—imprecise language, vague standards, and inconsistencies. For example, under the no-fault provisions of the Massachusetts plan, full medical payments for bills incurred within two years of an automobile accident is promised. However, the value of these medical services is described only by the word "reasonable." There is no price list for medical services, nor is there any objective standard by which the word "reasonable" can be interpreted.

The bill is inconsistent as well in awarding lost earnings. The commitment to pay three-fourths of one's lost earnings is based upon the injured's average earnings for the year preceding the accident. Unlike plans in other states such as Florida and Illinois, compensation for loss of profits suffered by businessmen forced to restrict or close their operations during convalescence is not included in the Massachusetts bill. Under the bill, it is possible for an unemployed victim to receive 100 per cent of his loss of earning capacity, whereas his employed counterpart gets only 75 per cent.

The substitute help provision also suffers from lack of clarity. The bill allows the injured the opportunity to obtain substitute help to perform the type of work he would have done but for the injury. There is no weekly limit to the compensation paid to the substitute and no standard suggested except, as in the case of the medical expenses, the amount paid must be "reasonable." Family members are excluded from this provision. The possibilities of litigation between the insured and the insurance companies over all these features are obvious. Differences of opinion are sure to arise over how these clauses should be interpreted.

Massachusetts has provided an option for deductibles of $250, $500, $1,000, and $2,000 to be applied against no-fault coverage. A deductible, as was noted, is an agreement between the insured and the company that the insured pay the portion of a loss equal to the amount of the deductible. In return, the insured receives coverage at a lesser premium. The insured is made a self-insurer for the deductible part of his loss. Since most drivers will not elect a deductible, it would be desirable to make the deductible feature a compulsory part of the no-fault package so as to eliminate the small claim.

Another anomaly of Massachusetts no-fault is the grant of immunity from tort liability. A person who is covered by no-fault cannot be sued in tort for an amount up to his own no-fault protection, if the person he injures is himself covered by no-fault. This means that an out-of-state driver coming into Massachusetts is still subject to a suit because he would not be covered by no-fault benefits. Conversely, the out-of-state driver is forced to sue even to obtain the $2,000 no-fault limit. But to succeed he must prove fault. The exemption has no correlation with the conduct of an individual but is based entirely on whether the party one is involved with has Massachusetts no-fault coverage. Despite the right to bring a lawsuit against an individual not covered, there is no opportunity to obtain general damages unless one of the six threshold exceptions is exceeded.

One of the celebrated goals of no-fault is to cut down on the use of the courts. But in many cases the number of lawsuits arising from automobile accidents is increased. No-fault, instead of eliminating litigation, at times, creates it. For example, a suit must be brought to recover the 25 per cent of wages left unpaid by the no-fault wage continuation benefit. This may be brought directly against the party causing the accident and is based upon fault. All economic losses that exceed $2,000 are recoverable in a tort action as are medical expenses that occur after the two-year limit for no-fault protection. All claims for general damage and wrongful death are potential lawsuits. Suit is still permitted for accidents happening outside Massachusetts, since the law of the place of accident is applied. There are several new types of actions permitted against those persons who are ineligible for no-fault and therefore without the immunity the statute grants. As for eliminating the use of the courts to determine matters in controversy, it must be stressed that not only is the right to sue retained, but it is actually expanded, except in the area of general damage claims, which include pain and suffering.

In any discussions of no-fault insurance, the term pain and suffering inevitably appears. Actually, the phrase is incomplete; general damages is a more appropriate description of this type of damage that includes, in addition to pain and suffering, emotional upset, loss of future economic ability, embarrassment caused by disfigurement, apprehension, and loss of enjoyment of life through a disabling injury. The nature of general damages is intangible and is not easily reduced to a specific dollar amount. Pain and suffering, or general damages, are not recoverable under no-fault unless the case falls within one of the six exceptions already listed. Massachusetts no-fault strikes out compensation for these damages in nearly all accident cases.

High on the long list of criticisms of Massachusetts no-fault is its own burdensome provisions, causing inconvenience to the insured. Personal injury cases are split into many parts. Some parts of the claim are collected from the driver's insurance company—the no-fault portion—and others are obtainable only on an adversary basis, as in the case of economic losses over $2,000. Because the case is split, all but the most persistent are discouraged from collecting what is fully owed. Confusion is the tactical ally of the insurer.

One of the overlooked concessions made by conversion to no-fault arises from the change of relationship that the

victim has with the insurance company. Now that automobile accident claims will be thrashed out between insurer
and insured, the victim's relationship with the insurance
company is as policyholder and not as adversary. Aside from
administrative conveniences, this means the company will
have more control over the conduct of the claim, and the
insured, less leverage in dealing with his own case. The
Massachusetts statute grants the insurers a new series of
defenses—reasons not to pay—which may be raised against
their own policyholders. For instance, the company can
refuse to pay medical bills when it decides they are unreasonable and unnecessary. Or the insurer can raise the defense that its policyholder did not cooperate with the terms
of his policy. According to the new law, the injured person
must give his own insurance company all details requested
about his wage loss and medical condition from every employer and doctor having information about the loss. The
company may demand a medical examination as often as it
deems necessary; the nature and extent of the physical
examination required is left unspecified by the statute. Furthermore, a claim for damages must be presented immediately after the accident occurs or the company can refuse
to pay on the grounds that the injured failed to give proper
notice.

Another paradoxical feature of the no-fault bill is its
provision for subrogation. Subrogation permits an insurance
company to recover no-fault payments made to its insureds
by collecting from the company insuring the person at fault.
Even though benefits are paid on a no-fault basis, subrogation depends on driver negligence. Insurance companies,
despite what was said by them in support of no-fault, were
eager to retain the fault system to evaluate their own risks
and to be reimbursed for the losses paid to those they insure,
based upon fault. Because of subrogation, fault must still

be determined in every case. No-fault does not end the importance of assessing liability in automobile accidents; it transfers the responsibility of that search from the injured to the insurance companies. Although the no-fault proponents have insisted that the search to find where fault lies in any automobile accident is futile, the insurance industry obviously disagrees and has retained an internal apparatus for determining fault.

To reinforce the necessity of fault-finding, the statute contains a limited merit-rating proposal. It allows a 4 per cent insurance discount for each two-year accident-free period. To the no-fault purist, the coexistence of a merit-rating system and no-fault are incompatible. If claims cannot be paid on a fault basis, why should risk be rated on a merit basis?

Notwithstanding all the efforts to restructure automobile insurance embodied in the Massachusetts bill, the greatest single failure was the retention of minimum liability limits at $5,000 per person, per accident. Despite the platitudes about the inadequacy of benefits going to those who are severely injured, nothing was changed to guarantee better coverage. The same inadequate coverage that existed before reform exists today.

Massachusetts no-fault, when applied to the nuisance and minor injury claims, does an adequate job. Its usefulness ends there. By pouring its resources into small claims, it leaves dangerously little for the seriously injured. Because it is difficult to define what is "serious," the Massachusetts statute has opted for as many objective standards as it could find, but these thresholds have been chosen on superficial and arbitrary lines, related to costs rather than human suffering. With the passage of time, cost must, as a matter of right, give way to what is equitable. In the meantime, it is an open question whether the motoring public is better off. Massachusetts will be the first state to know.

5
Pinnick's Complaint

AFTER MASSACHUSETTS GOVERNOR FRANCIS SARGENT signed the nation's first no-fault bill, its proponents and opponents girded themselves for the ultimate test. Would the state Supreme Court find no-fault constitutional? The antagonists did not have long to wait. The law took effect on January 1, 1971; on January 3, 1971, the "test case" accident occurred. For the first time in this country, the principle of no-fault automobile insurance was brought before a state court. The parties agreed in advance that the accident, a classic rear-end collision, was caused solely by the negligence of the defendant. It was further understood that the plaintiff, Irving Pinnick, would have been entitled to collect a settlement figure of $1,565, using the prior law as a guide, which included $115 as his reasonable medical expense for treatment of his injuries, $650 for loss of Mr. Pinnick's earning capacity derived from two jobs, and $800 allocated as payment for general damages, including pain and suffering.

Although it was a clear-cut case of liability, and one in

which Pinnick's damages ordinarily would have been paid to him without argument under the old system, the other party's insurance company declined to pay. Its defense: the new no-fault insurance act. Because the $1,565 could not be collected, Pinnick, through his attorneys, hastened to bring suit in the Supreme Judicial Court of Massachusetts to find out his rights under the no-fault statute.

The significance of this case was made clear at the outset. Usually, in order for a case to be heard by the Massachusetts Supreme Judicial Court, it must first be tried in a district or superior court and then appealed to the Supreme Judicial Court for an error of law. Not so for *Pinnick* v. *Cleary*. The plaintiff went directly to the Supreme Judicial Court to ask its opinion as to whether or not the no-fault bill was constitutional. The Supreme Judicial Court under certain circumstances may elect to accept such a case or decline it, depending upon whether it feels the issues are of sufficient public concern. In this case, because of the importance of either upholding or overturning the nation's first no-fault law, the court agreed to hear the case. Because the questions involved touched upon the entire issue of automobile insurance reform and were of such pressing public urgency, the court also agreed to extend its opinion beyond disposition of the narrow facts.

Representing the plaintiff was former Superior Court Justice Frederick S. Pillsbury of Springfield, accompanied by Alexander Cella and Robert Cohen, president at that time of the Massachusetts Trial Lawyers Association. Representing the defendant, Carl Cleary, was Herbert Wilkins, who for many years represented insurance company interests in Massachusetts. Briefs in support of the plaintiff were filed by the American Trial Lawyers, Massachusetts Trial Lawyers, and the Massachusetts Bar Association. Joining forces with the defendant in support of no-fault insurance were the American Mutual Insurance Alliance, the American Insurance Association, the Massachusetts Association of Independent Agents and Brokers, and the state's Attorney General's office. The adversaries were armed to the hilt.

It was agreed beforehand that Pinnick's case would have been worth $1,565 under the old system. What would he receive from no-fault? Under the new statute, Pinnick would no longer be eligible for any payment for his pain and suffering, because the case did not qualify as one of the six exceptions that allowed recovery for general damages. Pinnick did not have medical bills in excess of $500; nor did he have a fracture or a permanent and serious disfigurement; nor did he lose his sight or hearing as defined by the Massachusetts Workmen's Compensation Act; nor did he lose function wholly or partially of a bodily member; and, of course, he was not killed in the collision. Because he did not qualify on any of these six counts, he could not recover the $800 allocated for pain and suffering.

What about medical expenses? Under the old system, Pinnick would have been entitled to $115 toward medical bills, payable from the party who struck him or from the party's insurance company. The no-fault system made payment of his medical expenses recoverable from Pinnick's own company rather than from his opponent's.

On compensation for earning capacity, there was a sizable difference between the fault and no-fault provisions. The plaintiff in this case was a U.S. Post Office employee with a regular salary of $176.77 per week. As a result of the accident, he was absent seventy-three hours from work; he was paid in full by the Post Office by wage-continuation benefits from sick leave. Under no-fault, he could not collect from his own insurance company, because this amount was fully paid by the Post Office. Unlike the fault system, whereby Pinnick would have received his entire earning capacity in full from the negligent driver's insurance company, Pinnick was limited to recovery of three-quarters of his actual wage loss. But, under no-fault, any amount recovered from a collateral source, in this instance the Post Office wage-continuation program, was not again recoverable. But, as we shall see, the possibility of double recovery of wage loss was not totally cut off. Pinnick also had a second job giving him another $96.25 per week. In that job, he missed twelve working days and would, therefore, have been eligible to receive approximately $230 in addition from the fault system to compensate this second loss of earning capacity. Now he could expect to recover only three-quarters of this amount from his own insurance company. Because there was no wage-continuation program from Pinnick's second job, he could collect the entire claim.

The final tally under no-fault came to this: Pinnick could obtain from his own insurance company his medical bill of $115, plus three-quarters of $230 or $175.50 for his lost earnings from his second job. This meant that a total of $115 plus $173.50, or $288.50, was offered as a substitute for the $1,565 Pinnick would have received from the company insuring Cleary under the adversary system.

Pinnick's claim or "cause of action" was now split into several smaller actions. Whereas, under the old system, he would have obtained his entire damage in one claim against Cleary, he was now forced to make several claims. After exhausting his no-fault rights, Pinnick could then, if he persisted, institute a separate cause of action based upon fault against Cleary for the remaining $57.50, which represented the one-quarter of his earning capacity not recoverable under no-fault for his second job and not paid to him by his own insurance company. Although the statute is not clear on this point, the court in its decision indicated that Pinnick could have collected the full amount of his lost earning capacity even though his wages had been paid to him in full by the Post Office by instituting another claim against Cleary. These two items combined involving earning capacity losses from the separate jobs would allow Pinnick to bring an action based upon fault for a sum of approximately $477. This total equals the wages that were excluded from payment by no-fault, to be paid by Cleary's insurance company, should the suit be successful. Under no circumstances could Pinnick ever be compensated for general damages, because his damages did not qualify under any of the six exceptions.

What did the court think of this striking imbalance between what Pinnick could have collected under fault as compared to no-fault and how did it justify its position? The court held that the Legislature in enacting no-fault automobile insurance had changed the law only with respect to the amount a person could collect for damages. Compensation for pain and suffering or general damages was swept from the bill, except in extraordinary cases. In exchange for this loss of benefits, the victim gained new rights, while, at the same time, meeting his insurance needs at a lower cost. But, in the process of this exchange, what constitutional rights, if any, did the Massachusetts no-fault law violate?

First of all, the plaintiffs argued that the right of a victim to be fully compensated for pain and suffering and all other incidental and general damages due to someone's negligence amounted to a vested property right that could not be taken away from a citizen without a constitutional amendment. The court countered by reference to the landmark workmen's compensation case of *New York Central Railroad v. White*. This decision upheld the validity of the New York Compensation Law and announced the principle that no citizen owned a vested right in any rule of law that entitled him to insist that it should forever remain unchanged for his benefit. The court reasoned that a citizen may find his legal relationships altered by a new statute—his rights may be different before the statute than after—but he has no grounds for complaint simply because he finds the law has been changed to his disadvantage.

A second and related issue of federal rights was disposed of with equal ease. Was compensation for pain and suffering in cases of negligence guaranteed by the U.S. Constitution under a theory of protection of personal security and bodily integrity? The court stops short of saying that these rights do not exist at all but points out that, even if they do, the no-fault statute does not violate them. This law merely changes the traditional method of recovery in automobile accidents.

Here, the court recognizes that the Legislature must have the discretion and latitude to prevent the freezing of outmoded principles permanently into the legal system. In attempting to achieve this economic and social reform, the Legislature was free to alter existing rights. There is nothing in the Constitution that can be reasonably interpreted as meaning that the law cannot change.

Having disposed of the federal constitutional issue, the court now turned to state power. The court concluded that the Massachusetts no-fault law was passed by the Legislature within the rightful exercise of its police power. Once it is determined that a statute is properly within the exercise of that police power, the standard by which that statute is judged is whether or not it violates due process or equal protection. These two standards were applied by the Massachusetts Supreme Judicial Court to test the no-fault statute.

Due process is a legal term not easily defined. It has been said that due process means "that which is necessary to a state of ordered liberty." It has also been described as "that which is fundamentally fair." In passing on the due process issue, the Massachusetts court asked whether the no-fault statute was a step forward in the direction of insurance reform or a step backward from safeguarding individual human rights.

The court dealt with the principle of due process by saying it did not think the Massachusetts Legislature, in passing no-fault, had abolished any fundamental rights. Only one right was abolished: the right to collect damages from a wrongdoer for pain and suffering in those cases that did not fall within the exceptions allowed under the no-fault bill. The court pointed out that any other rights in effect prior to this reform legislation still remained but were enforced in a different manner. The court stresses here that the consequences of the no-fault insurance bill were not very significant as they only affected one part of the old system.

In this portion of the opinion, the court relied heavily upon an analogy with workmen's compensation statutes. As the "reasonable and adequate substitute" test was applied to workmen's compensation by past courts, the same test was applied to no-fault. Was the compensation now being offered by the Massachusetts no-fault statute a "reasonable and adequate substitute" for the protection previously available? The Massachusetts court concluded that, as far as due process was concerned, the plan amounted to a "reasonable and adequate substitute" for existing rights and, on that basis, was constitutional.

To justify no-fault as a reasonable alternative, the court went on to demonstrate how unreasonable the old negligence system had become. It began with the problem of court congestion. The key to understanding the entire decision is found in the statement by Justice Paul Cashman Reardon, the author of the opinion, who said: "The problems of society to which the courts have been called no longer permit the luxury of using them as a forum for resolving the ever increasing numbers of automobile accident claims to the extent that has obtained hitherto." By this remark, it is apparent that the court now wished to categorize automobile cases under a more convenient and less socially expensive form of claims handling. Left unanswered was why an automobile accident victim should be treated on a different basis than, for example, a person receiving a similar injury as the result of a fall on ice or as the result of a defective stairway. But it was made clear that the court was dissatisfied with the number of motor vehicle negligence cases that crowded the dockets.

No less troublesome was claims and accident frequency. Using statistical information from the years 1954 through 1956, which by the court's own admission was outdated, it noted the alarming frequency of personal injury claims in Massachusetts. The conclusion was drawn from that study that Massachusetts, in the area of bodily injury claims frequency per 100 cars insured, averaged two to three times the number of personal injury claims that occurred in the states neighboring Massachusetts. Comparisons showed that claims frequency in Massachusetts exceeded that in New York City for the year 1959 by 50 per cent. While the accuracy of these statistics may be challenged, it is interesting to speculate why the court did little else than list statistics without offering any further explanation of the factors causing such a disproportionate number of claims.

The court pointed out that the superior court was burdened with roughly 23,000 motor vehicle cases per year and that each case carried with it a companion pile of documents that took up a large amount of its time. But no mention is made of the need for more and better-trained personnel to accommodate the increasing volume of all varieties of litigation. In any case, the court used this "fact" of general congestion as a reason for favoring no-fault.

The court also launched into an analysis of the dollar amounts of jury verdicts. Using a set of statistics based upon the experience of the year 1956, the court inferred that most motor vehicle cases were small and cited as evidence in support of this conclusion that a similar amount of money would have been paid to the victim under no-fault. The court attempted to prove that the amounts of money awarded by juries as compensation to victims under the fault system were substantially the same amounts as these same victims could expect under a no-fault system.

This conclusion is hard to accept. As has been shown earlier, Pinnick would have received $1,565 under the traditional system of compensation, whereas under no-fault he was only entitled to his medical bill and three-quarters of his actual wage loss. His recovery under no-fault amounted to $288. It is difficult to agree with the court that the money received under the old system approximates the same monetary return to the claimant as he would receive under the new. The court goes on to say that Pinnick could recover further damages for the wages already paid to him by the Post Office through filing a separate suit. This is true of Pinnick's effort to obtain the one-fourth of his wages unpaid from his second job. Furthermore, his insurance company, having paid no-fault benefits, was allowed to arbitrate the issue of fault with Cleary's insurance company. It has not been determined whether, as a result of splitting one claim into several small parts, greater efficiency and less court congestion will result. While less money is involved in the initial claim, the no-fault bill, if anything, will increase the possibility of lawsuits, and for very small sums of money at that. A fair inference is that the drafters of this bill have deliberately made the money quest so unattractive by splitting the case that subsequent suits will be ignored by injured victims as being too cumbersome for the trifling amounts involved. As a question of policy, is this really fair to the traffic victim?

On one of the crucial points for seeking a "reasonable substitute" for the old automobile insurance—high cost to the
consumer—the court says virtually nothing. It does quote
from the U.S. Department of Transportation report on motor vehicle crash losses, mentioning that the fault compensation system has a higher ratio of cost to benefits than any
other compensation system in the country; that, in fact, for
every dollar of benefits going to victims, the system con-
sumes one dollar in administrative expense. But that is as
close as the majority opinion comes to entering a discussion
of the need for a reduction in insurance costs. High costs
apparently escaped the court's attention as a legitimate legislative objective to justify ending certain long-standing rights.

The court continued the no-fault drive to establish "rea-
sonableness" with a plea for convenience. It mentions the
weakness of delay in getting financial aid to the injured person when he needs it most. It points to the time and effort
spent requiring proof of fault, investigation of fraudulent
claims, false testimony, and the slow processing of claims.
The court agreed that no-fault was a rational approach to
the correction of these inadequacies but skipped over the
question of how the problem of delay by an insurance company or fraud by the public will be eliminated by the
statute.

The majority was satisfied to endorse no-fault as a reasonable substitute for the rights it took away by relying upon
the similarities to workmen's compensation and its exchange-
of-rights theory: The employee gives up his right to sue his
employer in exchange for the benefits he gains from workmen's compensation. A driver is always a potential victim
and at the same time the potential cause of an accident. In
no-fault, the driver gives up his right to sue in exchange for
the right to collect a smaller amount of compensation in *all*

accidents that involve him, even when he is at fault. The court approved this as being both just and convenient.

This conclusion makes sense except for one sorely neglected point. The court refused to distinguish between the different qualities of drivers. The decision does not treat good drivers differently from bad drivers but instead lumps all who operate motor vehicles into the same category. The court is saying that it is reasonable for the sake of cost and convenience to abandon fault; fault should not be considered in automobile accidents. The court, in a footnote to its opinion, said that "the day has long since passed when legal negligence in the automobile accident situation could be equated with moral culpability." This statement neglects driving under the influence of alcohol, drugs, or the willful violation of traffic laws, such as failure to observe stoplights or stop signs, or inattentive and careless driving that endangers human lives. Do not these instances of "legal negligence" involve "moral culpability"?

The exchange-of-rights theory was extended further to include the pedestrian. All drivers are at some time pedestrians, and the distinction between drivers and pedestrians disappears. The court points out that the pedestrian himself may be at fault due to his own carelessness and be ineligible for compensation under the negligence system. No-fault allows the pedestrian to recover in all cases even though the amount may be smaller than he could have collected previously. The court, in addressing the due process question, concluded that there had been no violation of that clause— the pedestrian had come away with a fundamentally fair deal.

The plaintiff raised the issue of compulsory insurance. Is it a reasonable requirement to force the consumer to buy automobile insurance from a private company before allow-

ing him to use the roads? In Massachusetts, there is no absolute right to drive a car on the public highway. Driving is
a privilege that can be given or taken away by the state. The
argument against compulsory no-fault was answered by the
court's saying that personal injury protection offered through
no-fault insurance becomes noncompulsory, because the policyholder is given the opportunity to purchase deductibles
with his policy so as to exclude himself from the no-fault
benefits as he chooses. The insured has the chance to self-
insure himself up to the limits of the deductible selected,
but he is left without a way to obtain the benefits lost by his
opting for a deductible.

The court goes on to say that, even if these deductible features were not offered, the Legislature in its wisdom by exercising its police power could demand compulsory insurance
for the good of society. Under the old system, compulsory insurance was for the protection of the other traveler. With no-
fault compulsory insurance, a driver protects himself—compulsory self-insurance—yet it is only obtainable from private
companies. The court indicates that the problem of a market
occupied solely by private companies is incidental to the
main issues and does not violate due process. Because private insurance companies are well regulated by state agencies, they are in a sense responsive to the public.

In a review of insurance rates, the plaintiff gets to the
heart and soul of his case. The rates charged in 1971 are
claimed to bear no reasonable relationship to the amount of
money needed to buy this type of automobile insurance.
The plaintiff felt that, by setting rates based upon tort
levels, while paying claims on a no-fault basis, the insurance
companies were taking money from him unfairly. Comparing Pinnick's recovery of $1,565 under the old system as
opposed to $280 under the new and pricing the rates of insurance on the same scale and at the same cost to the consumer,

the plaintiff's argument was sound. The court answered this by saying that, because this was an entirely new theory of automobile accident compensation and because there are no statistical data available to set rates accurately, the argument is invalid. The court urged insurance companies to extend a rebate payment to their customers, if they reaped a windfall profit in 1971 due to the vast reduction in claim payments. (The companies, thus far, have flatly refused to comply.)

The plaintiff in this case raised the objection that he was forced by no-fault first to look to his private wage-continuation program before applying for any payment for loss of earning capacity from his no-fault carrier. The court showed that no-fault insurance does not prevent him from obtaining his earnings a second time, by a suit based upon fault against the wrongdoer, even though they are paid from sources independent of automobile insurance. The court further states that the insured could now find himself in a better position to avoid double premiums for protection against similar losses. Premiums paid to Blue Cross and for overlapping protection to automobile insurance could be avoided by use of deductibles. Earlier in its opinion, the court said it would be well to carry duplicate coverages as a substitute for the loss of the right to sue for pain and suffering. The court in that portion of the opinion indicated that the accident victim would be assured of some profit over his out-of-pocket expenses incurred by a motor vehicle accident. This contradicts the earlier analysis of the undesirability of duplicate coverage situations. While no-fault proponents hail the elimination of duplicate coverage situations as a cost advantage of no-fault insurance, the Massachusetts Supreme Judicial Court goes off on an entirely different tangent, suggesting that overlapping coverage can supplement the system's compensation deficiencies.

Having tackled the due process arguments, the court turned its attention to the "equal protection" issues. Are there major differences in the treatment of various individuals, and, if so, do the distinctions serve a legitimate public purpose? Should the law provide for different categories of rights setting apart groups of people? And, if the law is permitted to group motorists, are the categories drawn along arbitrary, irrational, or discriminatory lines? This is the thrust of Pinnick's argument: that the criteria dividing the lines between those who are and those who are not eligible to be compensated for pain and suffering deny equal protection of the law.

The court countered by saying that a small claim involving pain and suffering is difficult to translate into objective standards. Due to this, the opportunity is ripe for fraud, creating a paradox where the expense of investigating such a claim exceeds its value. There is a history of overpaying nuisance claims to avoid the cost of defending against them. The court's reasoning comes to the conclusion that the Legislature was justified in eliminating the smaller pain-and-suffering claim because of the evils that surrounded them.

While this may be true, it is unsupported by fact or reason that a claim requiring $500 worth of medical attention should be dismissed as a nuisance claim and, conversely, that the presentation of a bill over $500 for medical attention should make an injury worthy of compensation for pain and suffering. The $500 medical threshold does not successfully serve as a cut-off between a nuisance and a non-nuisance claim. Many major injuries, particularly involving soft-tissue damage, may often fail to ring up a large medical bill.

The court conceded that the choice of an amount to carry the legal stamp of "threshold" must be arbitrary. But, as long as $500 was reasonable, it fits the bill as a threshold and was acceptable as a starting point to open the door to compensation for pain and suffering. In proving a narrow factual point—court congestion from automobile accident cases—the majority opinion traveled far abroad to obtain statistical evidence to buttress its finding. But, when it came to deciding the most crucial issue, the same type of investigation was not made. Instead of defending the premise that an injury lacking a $500 medical bill should be treated as a nuisance, the court says only that there was a definite need for a benchmark and $500 was as good as any. No other support was offered to justify this position.

Aside from being arbitrary, is the $500 threshold also discriminatory? To further the case that no-fault did not sin against equal protection, the court states that there is no evidence that poor people are discriminated against by their inability to reach the $500 plateau as readily as wealthier citizens. Again, the court did not make any independent inquiry to provide back-up information in support of this statement. When more data are available, a test of the $500 medical threshold must be made to bring it into conformity with sound cost-equity principles.

The two constitutional barriers of due process and equal protection collapsed. The court, through the majority opinion, declared that the no-fault automobile insurance bill was constitutional; the defendant was not liable to the plaintiff in an action of tort for negligence arising out of this accident. The majority opinion is an enthusiastic endorsement of the new insurance. It called motor vehicle negligence cases a "cancer" to be rooted not only from Massachusetts but also from the entire American court system. The court presents no-fault as a sure and appropriate step toward alleviating a motor vehicle accident compensation problem that had "defied more conservative solutions"—even though there was as yet no available experience to support this view.

As optimistic as the majority decision was in its endorsement of no-fault, the minority concurring opinion written by Chief Justice Joseph Tauro was sobering. Though agreeing with the result, his words were closer to outright dissent. He opened by conceding that Pinnick had failed to offer sufficient evidence to prove that he should have been compensated for the damages he sought, but noted that, under the circumstances, this would have been an impossible task. To go from this moot point to a firm statement that the Massachusetts Legislature had acted wisely in passing no-fault insurance was, in his opinion, premature.

For the first time in either opinion, reductions in the cost of insurance are mentioned. Tauro acknowledged that cheaper automobile insurance was a desirable objective, but, while supporting a cost reduction and the removal of some of the frivolous and fictitious claims for pain and suffering associated with automobile injuries, he did not wish to see "a burning down of the barn to get rid of the mice." The substitution of rights by no-fault as compared to the traditional methods of compensation is not as clear cut as the majority decision would lead us to believe. He indicated that Pinnick was entitled to $1,565 in damages under the old system, and that it would be difficult to convince anybody that $288.50 was a reasonable substitute.

The Chief Justice chided the majority for its oversimplified analogy of no-fault and workmen's compensation. Workmen's compensation established a new form of coverage that did not exist beforehand. When it was passed, none of the extant employee rights that had previously existed were removed by the Legislature. Workmen's compensation was and still is optional with the employee, and he may elect to retain basic common-law rights. The Massachusetts no-fault insurance does not allow the option of retaining common-law rights; these have been swept away. Moreover, the goals of the two statutes are different. Workmen's compensation was designed to protect employees against injury, not to reduce insurance costs or court congestion. Nor are classifications drawn among employees to create separate classes of those eligible to receive compensation. This is totally unlike the no-fault statute with its many categories and exceptions.

Although distinctions are made in awarding benefits by the no-fault bill, they are not on their face unreasonable, arbitrary, or prejudicial; this is the theme of the concurring opinion. But, in the absence of any further effort to make a rigorous fact-finding inquiry into the existence of arbitrary, irrational, or discriminatory features, the court is really in no position to go way out on a limb to endorse it. There is a possibility that, had more evidence been developed on this crucial consumer ruling, a different result could have been reached. The door is left wide open by the Supreme Judicial Court to return to issues, especially the minimum thresholds at which pain and suffering claims are permitted.

Chief Justice Tauro appeared to be frowning at the majority's application of statistical data to demonstrate the presence of court congestion, while, at the same time, presenting an empty ledger of the cost-equity analysis of this plan. He was dissatisfied with limiting recovery for pain and suffering to the six exceptions listed by the statute.

There is no evidence that the Legislature had made any investigation of the possible relationship between the extent of reasonable medical expenses and the legitimacy of a claim for pain and suffering. This fact was confirmed by the Legislature itself in openly admitting that the $500 threshold was chosen as a "good starting place." No indication was offered that the $500 level bore any correlation to "nuisance" claim avoidance, stated by the Legislature as its major purposes in passing no-fault. Tauro indicated that the majority, in passing a reasonable threshold, formulated its view in a fog of speculation and conjecture.

If these classifications are unreasonable, there is a serious constitutional defect in the no-fault act, due to the "equal protection" clause of the Constitution. Chief Justice Tauro offered a list of several serious injuries that cannot be reasonably defined as nuisance injuries but that are not exempted from the no-fault plan unless one of the six standard exceptions also applies. On this list, he included injuries such as torn muscles, tendons, and ligaments, sprained and dislocated joints, loss and dimunition of the sense of taste, loss of the sense of touch, loss of the sense of smell, rupture of a cervical disc, contusions of the brain, and other injuries to vital tissues and internal organs. Because these injuries cannot be characterized as nuisance claims and because they are excluded from compensation for pain and suffering unless an exception applies, the plaintiff wins this point. His equal-protection argument that the categories allowing exceptions from the restraints of no-fault limitations of compensation are arbitrary and unreasonable is basically sound, but it waits to be adequately documented in court.

On another score, Tauro challenged the contention that court congestion is due to accident litigation. The chief reason for court congestion is the rapid increase of criminal work, while the rest of the court's business waits. Accompanying this trend are other growing bodies of law gnawing their way into an overburdened system; these include consumer protection, malpractice, and product liability. The suggestion that motor vehicle negligence cases are a "cancer" is inaccurate. The trial of motor vehicle negligence cases is estimated to consume only about 11–13 per cent of the court's actual trial time. The no-fault statute will do little to change the percentage of time taken by automobile litigation in the superior court, because the claims that have been eliminated were normally tried in the district court or by a court-appointed auditor. Seldom was a nuisance case tried in superior court before a jury. There is little change in court volume due to this statute.

Chief Justice Tauro would have preferred to see the case of *Pinnick* v. *Cleary* sent back to the superior court for a full trial with more complete evidence. On the basis of the limited information that the court possessed, the Chief Justice reluctantly voted in favor of the constitutionality of the bill. The enthusiasm of the majority of the Massachusetts Supreme Court for no-fault suggests that it would be difficult for the court to reverse itself, but this does not mean that no one will try to induce it to do so. The concurring opinion goes far to pave the way for further questioning.

For the consumer and victim, the immediate effect of the decision is a lost opportunity to locate satisfactorily the optimum ratio of cost to equity. Future attacks on this statute are sure to be based on the lack of a good standard, because of which innocent victims are cut off from their right to sue for general damages including pain and suffering. As the law stands at the present time, there is room for amendment and improvement. If no-fault is to accomplish its positive mission of eliminating nuisance claims, more effort must go into defining what constitutes a nuisance claim. Until the proper balance of cost-savings and justice is achieved, there will be plaintiffs who are unfairly deprived of their right to full and fair compensation. Meanwhile, the decision rendered in *Pinnick* v. *Cleary* provides no-fault with a chance to live and to move ahead. Regardless of the quality of the court's opinion, this alone makes the case significant.

6
No-Fault Sweepstakes

DURING ITS FIRST YEAR OF LIFE, Massachusetts no-fault radically changed automobile insurance in that state. To no one's surprise, the first year produced an avalanche of statements and counterstatements about no-fault's success and failure. Because the partisans of no-fault had gone to such extremes to sell the program and because they were so wholly committed to its enactment, obvious shortcomings were swept under the rug. No-fault was shielded from criticism by its friends, but even some of its most ardent supporters now conceded the need for better performance.

Most of those who had opposed enactment of no-fault believed that, although court congestion (one of the reasons for the new bill) is undesirable, also undesirable are drastic reductions in benefits to innocent victims, removing the right to sue, and paying those who cause accidents. Such objections were based on philosophical ideas about what a socially responsible automobile insurance plan should be. Now, however, that a no-fault plan had been put into effect, the critics could examine whether it was actually achieving its goals.

No-fault proponents had criticized the fault system, saying it was an ineffective and inefficient means of distributing benefits, but they could never sell that argument. What they could sell was a reduction in cost to the insurance-buyer. In Massachusetts, the proponents of no-fault clearly built in a 15 per cent automatic cost reduction in compulsory personal injury coverage as part of the initial inducement for the Legislature to accept the no-fault package. The insurance companies rushed to pick up the ball and implied in their advertising that no-fault would result in a 15 per cent reduction in all related lines of insurance, such as property damage, collision, and comprehensive and medical payment. During the legislative debate, the 15 per cent reduction was in fact expanded to these types of automobile coverage, at which point the insurance companies threatened to leave Massachusetts. They unpacked their bags only after the Massachusetts Supreme Court abrogated the wholesale reduction and returned to the 15 per cent cut on compulsory personal injury coverage.

The 15 per cent reduction applies to only about one-fourth of the total automobile insurance bill. The public, led to believe it would pay 15 per cent less on total automobile coverage, now found its savings reduced. Furthermore, it was never adequately informed that, along with the cut, most of the benefits previously available under the fault system would be greatly reduced.

In 1970, approximately $622 million of combined automobile insurance premiums was collected by the companies writing in Massachusetts. Of this total, $153 million was collected for compulsory personal injury coverage—about one-fourth of the total income of the companies. The 15 per cent reduction was applied to this one-quarter. While the 15 per cent reduction did result in a saving for this one line of insurance, the other three-fourths were at the same time increasing. Property damage coverage went up during 1971 by 38.4 per cent over 1970, following the successful suit of the insurers to eliminate the 15 per cent across-the-board reduction given by the Legislature. To the consumer, this meant that, while personal injury compulsory coverage was going down, property damage premiums increased two and one-half times. Despite the passage of no-fault personal injury coverage, the total automobile insurance bill that the public was forced to pay was increased. In the end, profits soared and the consumer paid more and received less.

Even the 15 per cent reduction in personal injury coverage was actually very small for most Massachusetts motorists. Massachusetts, for the purposes of determining insurance rates, is divided territorially, with all its cities and towns broken down into one of fifteen rating districts. Within these fifteen districts, there are ten risk categories, making a possibility of 150 different rates for compulsory insurance. The lowest risk during 1970 paid a premium of $24 for compulsory insurance. Reducing $24 by 15 per cent meant that the motorist in this class realized a net saving of $3.60. During 1970, the average premium paid for compulsory insurance was about $65. Taking 15 per cent of the average figure, the decrease amounted to only $9.75 for the average insurance buyer. Professor Calvin Brainard of the University of Rhode Island Department of Economics dismissed this reduction by saying that 15 per cent of a molehill is a lot different from 15 per cent of a mountain.

When the time came to set 1971 insurance premium costs, the Massachusetts Insurance Commission protested that it lacked experience with rate-setting for no-fault coverage. It overlooked no-fault's similarity to health and accident coverage, which is designed to pay medical expenses and wage continuation. Because 95 per cent of negligence claims are wiped out by no-fault, what is left, in reality, are health and accident claims; it is difficult to imagine why this set of ratings was ignored. Instead, no-fault premiums were set, using the same rating base that applied to the fault system. A 15 per cent reduction was grossly insufficient. This figure was used despite the elimination under no-fault of compensation for pain and suffering in almost all accident claims, the elimination of virtually all attorney's fees, and the restriction banning the recovery of earning capacity in situations where other sources were available. It begins to be clear why the insurance companies challenged the 15 per cent across-the-board reduction but did not dispute the 15 per cent reduction as it applied to compulsory insurance. Profits for 1971 support their wisdom.

In setting a rate, the insurance commissioner must first add up the anticipated loss payments to determine a loss ratio—the percentage of the total premium dollar that will be paid for claims. The common figure for a loss ratio is 65 per cent of the entire insurance premium. In Massachusetts, due to its high claim frequency and high average claim payments, the loss ratio had crept up to over 70 per cent by 1970. The second factor used to compute the insurance premium is the expense ratio and includes acquisition costs, advertising, taxes, operating expenses, and profit. The usual expense ratio is 35 per cent, combining with the loss ratio to make the insurance dollar. As the loss ratio climbed above 65 per cent, the companies were forced to curtail the expense portion of the equation. The best way to cut expenses was by reducing acquisition costs, because the principal acquisition costs are those related to the brokers and agents. With the loss ratio rising, due to high claims volume, the stock companies curtailed these commissions as a way to balance the loss and expense factors. This accounts for the

insurance agents and brokers wanting to abandon fault for
no-fault; there was no ideological commitment to no-fault,
only the prospect of increased commissions.

A low profit margin, 1 per cent, is allowed by the insurance commission for selling compulsory insurance. Because
insurance is compulsory, and the automobile owner is forced
to buy this product, an artificial demand is created. On noncompulsory insurance, the profit level is generally left at 5
per cent. A good argument can be made for allowing no
profit at all on compulsory insurance. Even without a profit,
because the public is forced to buy this coverage, the companies would have the use of a tremendous pool for investment purposes, in what amounts to an interest-free loan, as
it does at present. Premiums are paid in advance by the insured, and the longer that claim payments are forestalled,
the greater the opportunity to use these funds as investment
capital.

The remainder of the expense ratio is consumed by operating expenses such as rent, salaries, and equipment. By
1970, the total loss ratio combining claims and expense factors rose to a figure in the neighborhood of 103 per cent.
Translated, this means that, for every $100 taken in by the
companies for compulsory personal injury insurance, $103
was paid out in the form of either claim payments or expenses. The result is an underwriting loss, which the companies point to to receive a rate increase for the following
year. But despite this paper loss, the companies still made
money. The companies were using the greatest part of $153
million in premiums to invest and reinvest. It is the return
on these monies, particularly when stock market conditions
are good, that resulted in the companies' operating in the
black for compulsory insurance. Due to the market decline
in the late 1960's, the companies by 1970 were no longer becoming rich on their investments. On the other hand, they

were not losing money on compulsory insurance. The net return on these investments still approximated 7½ per cent per year.

In summarizing the impact of investment return to the companies, Massachusetts Insurance Commissioner John Ryan said:

> Let there be no doubt that investment income deserves the attention given to it in recent years. It ought to be noted that on a national basis for the ten-year period between 1960 and 1969, the stock insurance companies showed a statutory underwriting loss of $1.3 billion before taxes, but an investment profit of $11.7 billion before taxes. These statistics help focus the issues. It shows that, even where no underwriting or insurance profits are earned, companies have the ability to make profits from money they receive from investors and premium payers.

When the rate-makers tried to set adequate and fair rates for a no-fault system, as we said, they used statistics based entirely on the performance of the tort system. In adjusting these figures for the anticipated impact of no-fault on the insurance rate, two calculations were made, both of which turned out to be wrong. The first inaccurate prediction concerned claims frequency. It had been anticipated that the changeover to a no-fault system would increase claim volume by 30 per cent, because of the additional number of injured motorists now eligible for no-fault benefits. No-fault, designed to pay everybody, included many individuals who had been disqualified, under the tort negligence system, by some legal barrier from successfully making a claim.

In 1971, instead of increasing, personal injury claims unexpectedly decreased by about one-third during the first six months of the year. In the first six months of 1970, the Massachusetts registry of motor vehicles recorded 76,160 personal injuries, while for the same period during 1971 it recorded only 48,906 personal injuries. The anticipated claims volume was off by about 50 per cent. The 30 per cent increase upon which the rate was set did not occur. Instead there was a 34 per cent decrease.

Three factors account for the sharp decrease. Undeniably, some of the missing personal injury claims were the result of no-fault's eliminating many of the outright fraudulent personal injury claims. It is impossible to estimate accurately the percentage of fraudulent claims, but they may have accounted for as many as 10 per cent of the total filed under the fault system. It is also believed that a significant number of victims injured in accidents were so confused about their rights under no-fault, because of the cascade of plans discussed in 1970, that, not knowing their rights, they failed to submit a report. The final factor and undoubtedly the most significant in this decrease was the unwillingness of the public to make personal injury claims against their own insurance policies, due to the long history of unfair cancellations and rate increases that it had come to expect from the companies. The insurance companies had successfully conditioned the public to the point where many preferred self-insuring small losses to running the risk of reporting the loss to their own insurance company.

The second critical miscalculation involved the amount of average payment per claim. Insurance companies set money aside as a reserve against future losses. For example, under the fault system in 1970, the companies put aside approximately $800 to cover the anticipated average claim payment. Before paying the loss, the money is held by the insurance company and invested for profit. Should the claim take four years to dispose of, the company can actually recover 30 per cent of the final payment—for example, on an average claim of $800, invested at 7½ per cent per year for four years, the company can earn back about $240. The reserves are later adjusted when the actual loss payments are known. But, because of the investment potential, there are advantages for the companies in keeping reserves high.

For setting reserves, the no-fault system made it difficult to determine the average worth of a claim. Because of the elimination of pain and suffering, legal fees, and payment of some lost wages, it was acknowledged that the average claim payments would decrease considerably. The commission predicted that the average claim payment would be approximately one-half of what it had been in 1970. If the average fault claim cost $800, the typical no-fault claim was to cost $400. This turned out to be dead wrong. The two pivotal predictions, then, were that (1) claims would increase by 30 per cent and (2) claim payments would decrease by about 50 per cent.

With the number of claims down by more than one-third from 1970, the anticipated average cost per claim also fell substantially lower. Unlike fault claims, which take longer to evaluate and become more expensive with time, no-fault claims are settled quickly and at more stable amounts. By applying fault principles to no-fault, the insurance companies overreserved: About 90 per cent of actual no-fault payments have been used to pay medical bills, with the remaining 10 per cent going for lost wages and substitute employment. The fact that economic losses are far more susceptible to investigation and control than intangible losses has led to a much lower average in claim cost than under fault. The average no-fault claim, paid during the first nine months of 1971, came in at a price of about $140 per claim—almost six times less than a fault claim during 1970, instead of the 50 per cent decrease projected.

The total average of all claims, fault and no-fault, for the same period amounted to $165. This illustrates the slight impact the handful of remaining fault claims had on the total average. Since both fault and no-fault claims were brought together, there are as yet no independent statistics available to separate the performance of the two systems.

Because of the two vital mistakes—claims volume and average claims payment—favoring the insurers, the companies collected much more premium than was warranted. During the first nine months of 1971, a total of 13,900 claims had been paid. These payments amounted to only $2.3 million, which is staggering when compared with the total premium intake of about $123 million. By deducting the expense ratio, which should have decreased due to a fall in claims volume, the companies were still left with a fund of about $80 million from which to pay claims. Even if every person injured during 1971 in Massachusetts had presented a claim to his insurance company for no-fault benefits, and the average of claim payments had risen from $165 to $200 million, the maximum conceivable amount payable from this fund would have been only $20 million. Even when increasing the average claim figure to $300, the maximum amount payable by the companies would be only $30 million, compared to the $80 million set aside for claims payments. While it will be a number of years before reserves are adjusted to losses, a conservative estimate of the companies' profits lies in the range of $50 million. And this figure does not take into account any income earned on investments of reserves.

In setting the 1972 rate, Commissioner Ryan acknowledged that the 1971 compulsory personal injury rate had been excessive by at least 27.6 per cent, an admission by the regulatory agency that the Massachusetts motoring public had been overcharged by the insurance industry by about $35 million during 1971. Even the most ardent supporters of no-fault, including former State Representative Michael Dukakis, felt this figure was unduly conservative in view of the loss experience to date. In any event, in 1971, the insur-

ance companies made a killing. One wonders whether or not
the industry, with its staff of financial wizards and actuarial
merlins, could have been honestly mistaken. One suspects
that, during the no-fault debate, the companies knew well
that the Massachusetts version would bring them enormous
profits. Is it any wonder that, on the basis of what has been
given them in Massachusetts, the industry is strongly pro-
moting no-fault in other states?

In 1971, the Massachusetts Legislature passed a law that
provided that the companies, in a year in which excess profits were earned, could be required by the Commissioner to
set aside funds to be redistributed in the following year in
the form of reduced premiums. Relying on this statute,
Commissioner Ryan ordered that the companies set aside a
fund equivalent to 35 per cent of the 1971 compulsory insurance premium for a possible rebate. To quote Commissioner
Ryan, "The facts tell us quite clearly that compulsory insurance rates for 1971 could have been cut at least 42 per cent
rather than 15 per cent and still have been adequate, just,
reasonable, and nondiscriminatory, as the law requires them
to be. Rather simply, this means that the government was
wrong a year ago; it could have done more in cutting rates
than it did." Unfortunately for the public, the "look back"
statute is generally believed to be unconstitutional, because
it requires taking from the companies monies already earned.
Under principles of constitutional law, this amounts to con-
fiscation of personal property without due process.

The motorist did receive a token premium decrease. The
average premium before no-fault was $65, which, when re-
duced by 15 per cent for 1971, brings the total down to $55.
In 1972, there was a further reduction of 27.6 per cent,
bringing the average cost down to about $40 per policy.
How insignificant both these decreases were is obvious when
evaluating the kind of protection available from no-fault

coverage. In 1970, the fault system returned about 70 per cent of $153 million in loss payments to accident victims. This amounted to approximately $117 million. Applying the Keeton-O'Connell formula embodied in the original no-fault plan, which says that only $.44 of every premium dollar taken in by the fault system is returned to accident victims, Massachusetts victims still would have received about $67 million in payments based on the 1970 premium. Comparing this to what happened under no-fault, we see that, for a premium reduction of 15 per cent, Massachusetts drivers received only $2.3 in claims payments for the first nine months in 1971. Even if we speculate that every person injured in Massachusetts in automobile accidents during 1971 will receive an average of $200 per claim, the highest total payout possible would amount to $20 million. Whereas average rates were decreased by a ratio of three-to-two, benefits were taken away by a ratio of over five-to-one. To state it another way, the 42.6 per cent reduction for the years 1971 and 1972 resulted in about an 80 per cent loss in benefits.

Despite all that has happened to the advantage of the insurance industry, a further hidden increase was inflicted on the Massachusetts motoring public. Massachusetts, as we have mentioned, is divided into fifteen separate rating districts. In 1972, the towns within this rating system were rearranged. A total of 276 out of 351 towns moved into higher-paying brackets. Some cities, such as Springfield, jumped up as many as three notches. Only eleven cities and towns were classified into lower-paying brackets. None of the cities and towns that were lowered had their rates reduced by more than one rating zone. As a result of this shifting, the 42.6 per cent reduction in the cost of personal injury coverage amounted to even less for those consumers who happened to live in a city or town that was moved to a higher rated zone.

In establishing the 1972 rate, once again the mistake was made of setting the price for no-fault insurance on a fault base. No-fault must be separated entirely from the negligence claims, since, for rating purposes, they have different characteristics. This will avoid overreserving, which led to the inflated rates of 1971 and 1972. When passing on the 1972 rate, Commissioner Ryan predicted an increase of 20 per cent in personal injury claims over 1971, ignoring the 34 per cent drop in claims that actually took place during 1971. On the basis of the 1972 rates, the insurance industry will collect about $90 million in compulsory no-fault personal injury premiums. In view of 1971 profits, we must conclude that setting the price of compulsory premiums this high is unduly protective of the industry.

No-fault has failed the consumer on yet another score. It has been advanced as a way of getting payments to the traffic victim very soon after his injury. That traffic victims suffer great delay before money is paid to them is widely accepted. But no-fault is running into the same difficulty. During the first nine months of 1970, the fault system was able to originate and close 26,906 cases. For the same period in 1971, no-fault was able to originate and close only 13,900 claims, or about 50 per cent fewer.

Perhaps both systems are inherently slow for reasons beyond the scope of any legislation. No-fault systems depend on reports from various independent people before payments can be made. The worst offenders in creating this kind of delay are the medical people. Until a medical report is submitted, there is absolutely no way that the companies will undertake to establish what benefits are due. There is nothing about no-fault that will persuade the doctor to send his report in sooner. The same is also true of wage reports. Until a statement is received from an employer under either system, no evaluation can be made of wage payments owed.

These factors, the medical report and the wage confirmation, consume equal amounts of time regardless of which system is in effect.

Whereas the passage of no-fault personal injury insurance generated acrimonious debate, the Massachusetts compulsory no-fault property damage law, passed late in 1971 to place all automobile insurance on a no-fault footing, passed unobtrusively. Most likely, the trial lawyers who had bitterly opposed no-fault compulsory personal injury coverage, out of frustration, did not attempt to block the property damage reform. According to this new law, for the first time, Massachusetts makes its automobile owners carry compulsory property damage. It is only nominally no-fault. Claims for damages to automobiles arising out of accidents with other Massachusetts motorists are barred, because, by purchasing this policy, motorists are given a complete exemption from suits against them by other drivers, regardless of fault. If two cars collide at an intersection, neither driver can sue the other for property damage. Both are forced to make claims for their damages to their own insurers.

The insurance purchaser is required to choose one of three compulsory options. If he does not, he is not allowed to register his automobile. The first provides for coverage similar to what was formerly known as collision insurance. The purchaser of this option is given protection against all damage done to his car without regard to fault. Should he run off the road and strike a stone wall, he is still paid for the damages to his car. He is also given total immunity from suits brought against him by other drivers who are covered by Massachusetts no-fault. In addition, he gets protection against suits when he is out of state and subject to the liability laws of other jurisdictions. One feature of this option is that automobiles are rated for premiums with respect to their damage potential. Since an expensive car is a greater risk, owners of late model automobiles can expect healthy rate increases for this kind of coverage.

The second option provides coverage that is comparable to property damage insurance available under the old system and designed to repair damage caused by the insured to other automobiles. The purchaser of the second option now must make a claim to his own company, but he can recover only when he can show that the other driver was at fault. If the insured was the cause, although he buys this option, he cannot recover.

Thus, for example, if two cars collide at an intersection and the insured is judged to be 100 per cent responsible, his own insurance company, acting under the second option, would not be liable for any payment. If the insured were found to be 25 per cent responsible under the Massachusetts comparative negligence statute, the insured would receive 75 per cent of his total damage; if damage to the car was $800, the company would offer $600. Any disagreements between company and insured would be settled in court. It is this second option that will inevitably produce a torrent of litigation because it is sure that the insureds and the insurers will disagree as to the amount of payment owed.

The final option provides no coverage whatsoever to pay for the damage caused to the insured's own automobile, through either fault or no-fault. All it does is to protect the insured against potential lawsuits brought against him in those rare situations when a tort action for property damage is still allowed. The coverage offered by this option applies only to out-of-state accidents, accidents within Massachusetts involving property other than damage to automobiles, and accidents within Massachusetts with out-of-state cars or governmental cars, which do not have to carry no-fault property damage. These cases are few and far between.

In 1971, the cost of property damage coverage rose by

38.4 per cent, after the insurance companies' successful lawsuit overturned the 15 per cent across-the-board reduction. In 1972, a further increase of about 10 per cent was added. In two years, the cost of property damage increased by nearly 50 per cent over the cost in 1970. In 1970, premiums in Massachusetts amounted to about $140 million for property damage, which protects other people's property, plus $177 million for physical damage coverage, which protects the insured's own automobile. The 1970 total is $317 million for combined property damage coverages. In 1972, the costs rose to approximately $475 million—an increase of $158 million.

The final indignity thrust on the public is the cost of the third option. Coverage under this option is 70 per cent less than the 1971 property damage rate. This appears to be a major saving until one sees that the charge, which amounts to 30 per cent of the 1971 rate, protects the insured for nothing. He is forced to buy this coverage, it is compulsory—he cannot drive his car without it. Keeping in mind that tort suits under Massachusetts no-fault property damage are forbidden against other Massachusetts drivers, the captive purchaser of this coverage is left without a means of getting money to repair his car even when he is blameless. He gets nothing from his own company; nor can he sue. He is paying 30 per cent of the 1971 property damage rate for virtually zero benefits.

It will take several years to measure the total economic impact of no-fault. Early returns in Massachusetts, however, show that the companies have made an unconscionable profit and that the insurance-buying public in 1972 is paying considerably more for inferior coverage when compared to costs and benefits available under the fault system. Clearly, the political opportunism of 1970 has led the consumer down the garden path.

7
From Oregon to the
New York Island

FROM THE FIRST PASSAGE of a no-fault bill in Massachusetts, the movement for insurance reform crossed into Florida, Delaware, Oregon, and Illinois. Within weeks, each of these states was driving hard to pass its own version of no-fault legislation. The bills differed, with some states adopting features that others ignored. Meanwhile, other states were either rejecting no-fault or recommending further study. Whatever the motivation for switching to no-fault, no state saw fit to pass a total no-fault bill that would eliminate all possibilities for negligence claims, including the right to be compensated for pain and suffering.

Although the total no-fault approach so far has been avoided by the states, each direction taken has led to widely varying consequences for both the victim and consumer. For example, Oregon's bill is extremely liberal in its retention of claims based upon fault and uses no-fault as a supplement.

Other states, notably Florida, pay lip service to claims for damages based upon fault and have imposed such high thresholds as to exclude most possibilities of law suits from traffic accidents; pain and suffering has been eliminated as a significant compensation factor in auto insurance. If a pattern has developed at all, the various states have gravitated toward a dual system that seeks to achieve balance between fault and no-fault principles.

The insurance industry, supported by Professor Jeffrey O'Connell, has expressed doubts about the ability of any dual system to accomplish the goals of no-fault insurance reform. O'Connell fears that the dual system now evolving will cause a rise both in claims frequency and in costs, because no-fault opens the door to everyone injured in automobile accidents to present claims. In addition, both he and the insurance industry contend that the fault system, with its rising administrative costs, when combined with a no-fault system, would inevitably push premiums upward.

By passing dual systems, the states have swung the pendulum away from total no-fault's preference for cost over equity. If total no-fault can be criticized for ignoring fairness to the victim while favoring cheaper automobile insurance, the reverse is true of the more liberal dual systems. Cost concern has been de-emphasized to provide more compensation to the accident victim. Difficult decisions must be made to select the midpoint between the tight-fisted approach designed to please the consumer and the "pay everyone everything" plans motivated by the humane desire to compensate all accident victims fully and fairly.

Because the no-fault programs now in motion differ from state to state, it is impossible to make generalized statements that apply to each plan. For the sake of convenience, however, there are five broad categories into which automobile insurance reform can be pigeon-holed. The first type of no-fault package and the most extreme is the "total no-fault plan," advocated by the American Insurance Association, the trade association of insurance stock companies, and the State Insurance Department of New York. In this scheme, the concept of fault in automobile accidents is completely eliminated, except in case of death and when the insurance companies subrogate or redistribute claim payments. But the plan does have broad no-fault provisions. No-fault protection, besides covering the small and intermediate claim, offers compensation for the catastrophic injury as well.

The total no-fault approach represents the ultimate effort by the insurance industry to make the compensating of accident victims entirely objective. It says that, because intangible damages are hard to compute and difficult to prove, they should be dropped. In so doing, the plan exposes its fundamental flaw. Often the greatest loss in an accident can not be measured by neat mathematical formulas. A man with a desk job could lose a leg in an accident without impairing his earning capacity, but certainly an injury of this severity has a value beyond economic loss.

Before slamming the door on total no-fault, the much publicized advantage of such a plan deserves a hearing. With respect to compensation for economic losses arising from automobile accidents, payment potential is high. All medical expenses would be paid in full, all wages lost would be paid during the time of total disability for an unlimited length of time, though the maximum monthly payment is pegged at $750. As a second advantage, its proponents insist that automobile insurance would be less expensive, because, by skipping the courts, a higher percentage of the money injected into the insurance system would go directly into the victim's pocket. Because insurers could better take into account how much a customer will cost the company in the event of a claim, insurance premiums can be computed more accurately. This would revolutionize underwriting: A potential risk would no longer be considered in light of his likelihood to cause an automobile accident but would be rated instead on his potential as an economic loss. Limitation to recovery of economic losses makes for a highly predictable risk, a factor that has enormous appeal to the insurance industry. The heady profits made in Massachusetts by the insurers in 1971 has whetted their appetite to promote a total no-fault plan.

But there are danger signals. The extension of a total no-fault plan to all victims injured in automobile accidents on an unlimited basis will result in short-term cost savings, but, should the system become expensive, benefits would take a plunge. With a drop in benefits, we would be left with insurance that cuts off the seriously injured without adequate compensation and that would be efficient only in providing for very small claims. All signs indicate the plan should be abandoned. Made lopsided by its insistence upon objectivity, compensation for human suffering is ignored as a worthy component of the plan. Fortunately, the total no-fault approach has never been adopted, although New York State is seriously considering total no-fault, with Governor Nelson Rockefeller's blessing. As Daniel Webster warned, "An honest man should not sleep while the state legislature is in session."

The second category of no-fault plans is the now familiar Keeton-O'Connell "basic protection" type introduced in chapter 1. This plan keeps within its boundaries at least the slight prospect of a victim's being able to make a claim based on negligence and, in a limited way, retains the concept of fault for the extremely serious case. The plan permits claims for pain and suffering and other general damages based upon fault only if losses exceed a threshold of $10,000. This proposal assists the catastrophically injured by guaranteeing at least $10,000 for payment of economic losses, regardless of fault.

The original version of the Keeton-O'Connell bill insisted that the victim initially exhaust all of his private medical resources as well as income from other types of insurance and sick leave programs before the no-fault benefits could be drawn upon. This meant that automobile insurance was dependent on non-automobile-insurance sources for its savings, in particular, private insurance plans, which are having their own difficulties with rising costs. It was criticized on the grounds that, although using automobile insurance as secondary rather than primary protection would drive the cost of automobile insurance down, the savings would be eaten up in the hidden costs of private health insurance increases and additional burdens on wage-continuation plans. The "basic protection plan" was labeled parasitical and was bitterly opposed by trial lawyers, private health insurers, and organized labor, among other groups.

Keeton-O'Connell has been rejected for its insistence upon high thresholds before allowing pain and suffering claims. These thresholds are so unrealistically high that intangible damages could almost never be recovered. Were this plan enacted, it is likely that 99 per cent of all claims for intangible damages would be eliminated. A fair analysis of the "basic-protection plan" discloses equity has been sacrificed for cost.

Since "basic protection" was first announced and considered in 1967 by the Massachusetts Legislature, the authors have doctored their plan considerably. It now includes a choice of purchasing no-fault insurance or remaining subject to the law of negligence. It operates as follows: Each insurance-purchaser would have an option to buy a no-fault, "basic protection" policy, to protect himself and other members of his household, authorized drivers of his car, and guests for their out-of-pocket expenses up to $10,000. As part of the bargain, he would give up the right to sue the person causing his damage. The second option allows a choice. Those who wish to continue within the present liability framework without the "basic protection" benefits may do so. Those who prefer no-fault may buy this policy. The double option says: Let the two systems compete; let the fault devotees go one way and the no-fault another way.

Suppose that driver A and driver B have an accident. If neither chose to carry the Keeton-O'Connell no-fault option, a traditional negligence claim for full damages based upon fault would be permitted for both. If A happened to carry no-fault coverage but B did not, A would receive no-fault benefits from his own company; B would get nothing from his own company but would be free to make claim against A based on tort for negligence. As part of A's no-fault insurance package, in addition to receiving no-fault benefits if he were injured, he would be given liability coverage to defend and pay any claim brought against him by B. The unique feature of the double option proposal is that, instead of the cost saving's being realized by B's insurance company, because A has forgone his right to sue, the savings from the plan would flow into a fund that would be used to lower insurance costs for those drivers who elected to buy the no-fault option.

Incentive is given to a consumer to buy this form of protection, because benefits are paid automatically, regardless of fault at a cost reduction made possible by the pooling device. The plan has merit. On the plus side, it allows two systems to compete in the market place, giving the consumer greater choice in the purchase of automobile insurance. On the minus side, it drives up administrative costs by requiring that a double system be maintained.

The plan passed by Massachusetts and later by Florida

fits most closely into this second category, the Keeton-O'Connell prototype.

As compared to Massachusetts, Florida's version of the no-fault act is considerably more restrictive in allowing claims based upon fault and the recovery of damages for pain and suffering. Conversely, the Florida plan is more generous than Massachusetts in awarding no-fault benefits:

• Medical payments and disability benefits carry a limit of $5,000 rather than the Massachusetts $2,000 limit.

• The victim is reimbursed for 85 per cent of his actual lost wages in Florida, as opposed to 75 per cent in Massachusetts.

• Florida adopts the substitute-worker provision, permitting the injured party to hire someone to perform his work during the time of convalescence.

• The Florida version has included $1,000 per person for funeral expenses in fatal accidents.

• To assist the victim during the time he needs money most, Florida, unlike Massachusetts, has required that the company pay the benefits due at intervals not greater than every two weeks.

• In Massachusetts, the threshold used to allow tort recovery is $500, while Florida doubles this to $1,000.

• Massachusetts will allow recovery for pain and suffering based upon fault for any fracture; Florida, before granting an exception, limits the fracture to a weight-bearing bone. Massachusetts by failing to be more definitive has sent trial lawyers scurrying to their medical dictionaries. The broader the interpretation given to fracture, the greater the possibility for a general damages claim.

• The Massachusetts plan has been criticized for barring individuals who receive free medical assistance—such as members of the armed forces—from collecting for their pain and suffering, because it is impossible to present a medical bill of $500. Florida recognizes this difficulty and solves it by permitting individuals who receive free medical attention to include the fair value of this assistance in reaching the $1,000 threshold.

• The Florida statute goes far to assist the insurance industry to investigate claims brought against it by policyholders. In Florida, the insured's employer is compelled to make a sworn statement of his employee's earnings to assure that the amount of lost wages claimed is valid. Every physician, hospital, and medical institution is required to provide full reports to the insurance company concerning the policyholder's complete medical history, condition, and treatment.

Both the Massachusetts and Florida approaches center on locating a minimum threshold, before claims for pain and suffering and other intangible damages are permitted. In this respect, they are faithful to their mentor, the original Keeton-O'Connell plan. Each plan is considerably short of perfection, but, weighing the many efforts at insurance reform, this approach might ultimately prove best. At present, the threshold amounts are no more than arbitrary figures pulled out of a hat and elevated to legal status. With time and experience the thresholds could be adjusted to correlate better with actual injuries. The key to success, then, lies in a better choice of a minimum threshold, and, if these plans are economically successful, reducing the threshold to allow for a wider spread of benefits.

Unlike Massachusetts, where property damage was not considered on a no-fault basis until a year after the original bill passed, Florida took on this closely related issue at the outset. Property damage is not compulsory in Florida but is made available on a no-fault basis at the motorist's option. The plan is a strange conglomeration of rights. An individual licensed and registered in Florida is exempted for the damages he causes to others, if the damage does not exceed $550. When damages exceed $550, the fault system becomes operative. If the $550 figure is surpassed, a tort claim based upon fault may be brought to include the full amount of the damage.

Within this option, Florida divides its property damage reform proposal into two separate plans. One is called "full coverage," which is a no-fault plan similar to what was formerly called collision insurance. The other is "basic coverage," which is limited to claims for damage caused by the fault of another. If "full coverage" is chosen, property damage is paid in full, regardless of fault. If "basic coverage" is chosen, property damage is still paid by one's own company but only if fault can be shown on the part of the other driver. Under both options, the claim is presented to the driver's own company; one uses fault and the other no-fault. If no property damage insurance is purchased, suits against the other driver are forbidden, unless the damage exceeds $550.

The third category of no-fault bills is the type passed by Illinois and under consideration in Pennsylvania. An outgrowth of the Cotter plan, it has been endorsed by the American Mutual Insurance Alliance, the trade organization of the mutual companies. In it, two separate systems operate side by side: Minimum no-fault benefits are guaranteed, while the fault system is kept alive by imposing restrictions on compensation for pain and suffering.

• The Illinois plan provides that no-fault medical benefits be offered to a limit of $2,000 per person per accident.
• It offers 85 per cent of lost earning capacity to a limit of $7,800 payable in maximum installments of $150 per week. The wage provision includes the right to claim the

loss of profits, when the victim is forced to close or restrict
business activities because of his injury.

• Illinois carries a substitute-help provision to pay individuals who perform services for the injured during the time
of convalescence and offers $12 per day for one year for this
help.

• The insurer is required to offer to each policyholder the
chance to buy an excess no-fault policy of $50,000 per
person per accident, and $100,000 per total injuries per
accident. The option is given to buy unlimited medical coverage, income continuation to $39,000, substitute-help bene-
fits of $12 per day for five years, and $2,000 for funeral
expenses all on a no-fault basis.

This plan offers both mandatory and optional no-fault features and provides for the recovery of noneconomic or intangible losses, including payment for pain and suffering,
mental anguish, and inconvenience. The Illinois statute retains the right to sue for negligence, but with limitations on
how much can be collected. In those cases where the reasonable medical expense is less than $500, the pain and suf-
fering or general damages recoverable is limited to half of
the medical bill. For example, if a man is injured in an automobile accident and must pay $400 to his doctor for medical
expenses, the maximum amount of money recoverable for
pain and suffering is $200. If his medical expense exceeds
$500, he can receive an amount equal to the total of his
medical bill. Should his medical bill be $600, he is entitled to
an additional $600 for pain and suffering, if he can prove
this damage and if he can show someone else was at fault.

The Illinois statute cuts into court congestion by imposing
mandatory arbitration of small cases, which are defined as
claims in which $3,000 or less are in dispute. This is a high

point of the statute. It tries to reduce pressures on the courts by taking from them the smaller disputes, though preserving a person's right to make such a claim. To put teeth into the Illinois arbitration clause, the parties are encouraged to agree in advance that arbitration is final and, by so doing, eliminate further resort to the courts.

The Illinois law contains a lengthy section (absent from other no-fault statutes) on fraudulent claims that could serve as a model for discouraging these practices. The penalties, including revocation of driving privileges, apply not only to the person directly benefiting from the exaggerated claim but also to those who assist him.

But the Illinois plan has missed the mark in its effort to convert intangible damages into rigidly defined objective standards by connecting them to the medical charges. The question remains whether the amount of general damage suffered in an accident bears a relationship to the total of the victim's medical bill. As we concluded earlier, the man with an expensive doctor, who demands the best in medical services, will fare much better under this plan than his poorer counterpart. Not only does he receive better attention, but, at the same time, it enhances the possibility of full compensation. Taking this a step further, the Illinois reform encourages the exaggeration of medical expenses, because the higher the medical bill, the higher the reward. This system indirectly imposes an unneeded burden upon medical facilities by inviting their increased use.

The Illinois plan can also be criticized for emphasizing the smaller claim. One of the pressing concerns of accident reform is the elimination of overpayments to victims who were not seriously injured. Why, then, should a $50 medical bill be followed by a pain-and-suffering award of $25, as permitted by the Illinois statute? This smaller type of claim should be abandoned altogether, for the sake of cost, or given to a total no-fault handling, rather than offering a token payment for general damages while employing the fault machinery to do so. The Illinois package has the built-in disadvantage of squandering no-fault strong points. In its effort to control claim costs, Illinois relies upon an irrelevant comparison of medical expense and injury severity as the measure of general damages claims. Though its purpose is to cure the ills of the fault system and so to avoid the grim possibility of total no-fault, as a compromise it fails.

Since its passage, the Illinois bill has been challenged on constitutional grounds and its future is in doubt. Its opponents bring the charge that it fails to satisfy equal protection standards of the Illinois constitution, because it discriminates against the poor by linking the amount of pain and suffering to the victim's medical bill.

A fourth route to automobile insurance reform was taken by the states of Oregon, Delaware, and South Dakota, again supporting dual fault and no-fault systems—as in the case of Illinois, but with major differences. The Illinois system uses no-fault reform to alter extensively and restrict the law of damages. The Oregon-Delaware-South Dakota no-fault plans leave the fault system of compensation for damages entirely intact and supplement it with partial no-fault. This method leaves everyone in at least as good a financial position as he was before no-fault.

As an example, the Oregon scheme works as follows:

• On a no-fault basis, the plan provides for a medical payment of $3,000 per person per accident.
• The victim is guaranteed 70 per cent of gross earnings, limited to $500 per month, with a $6,000 limit payable without regard to fault.
• No claims can be paid before the end of a fourteen-day

waiting period following an accident. This is a positive feature designed to eliminate some smaller claims.

• The substitute-help provision is used, which will pay 100 per cent of the cost of substitute labor under no-fault to a limit of $4,300.

• Any benefits paid by no-fault are returnable to the no-fault insurance-carrier, if there is a subsequent recovery from a successful fault claim. No-fault is supplementary and is used to deliver benefits to the victim at his most urgent time of need, without abandoning the tort system.

• The Oregon no-fault protection is extended to the insured, his family, guest passengers, and pedestrians, though not to persons eligible for workmen's compensation. Guest passengers and pedestrians may apply the no-fault coverage only as excess coverage to pay expenses not covered by their own collateral resources.

• No-fault benefits paid under this plan are deducted from any future liability claim to prevent double recovery of fault and no-fault compensation for the same damages.

The Oregon statute is designed to pay economic losses immediately. Once economic help is extended, the victim retains the right to sue just as he did before the no-fault reform. Should he win, the individual can only recover what he was not already given by no-fault; should he lose, the victim still retains the no-fault payment. According to this scheme, no-fault is merely an advance payment precedent to a claim based upon proof of negligence.

At the same time that no-fault passed in Oregon, companion legislation improved the fault system by eliminating contributory negligence (the victim, when a little bit at fault, recovers nothing), substituting for it comparative negligence (the victim, when not more than 50 per cent at fault, can recover at least a fraction of his damages). With comparative negligence, money recovered in tort cases will be given on a proportioned scale based on the percentage of fault assigned to the victim.

Oregon has kept a full liability system and superimposed upon it partial no-fault, which may increase insurance costs and claims frequency. The financial performance of Oregon in the years to come will be watched with great interest; the plan, except for its potential costs, is the most equitable proposed to date. Allowing everyone injured to be eligible for the no-fault provisions, plus retaining the tort reparation system, promises an increase in automobile insurance premiums. Nevertheless, the Oregon experiment is a step in the right direction. By its passage every accident victim in Oregon knows that he will receive economic compensation for his injuries and will not be deprived of the opportunity to make a liability claim in cases where there are significant intangible losses. If it happens that the availability of no-fault benefits results in a cost-saving in insurance due to the voluntary abandonment of small fault claims, the Oregon plan would combine the best of both worlds.

The Oregon plan along with those adopted by Delaware and South Dakota have been dubbed by no-fault proponents as phony no-fault plans. The reformers have complained that these three states have stretched the definition of no-fault to a point where it no longer can be recognized. Oregon seeks to prove that the less spectacular solutions for automobile insurance reform are possible, short of going the whole no-fault route. For those who favor the adversary system, this plan is a last chance to reverse the rush to no-fault.

The four categories mentioned represent automobile insurance offered on a partial or full no-fault basis under the aegis of private insurance companies. The fifth group represents a governmental or quasi-governmental takeover of the role of the insurer. Two pilot plans putting this idea into effect are already under way in Puerto Rico and Saskatchewan. The Puerto Rican plan, called "Puerto Rico Automobile Accident Social Protection Act," instituted on January 1, 1970, is administered directly by the government. The plan is financed by a compulsory car registration fee that supplements an insurance pool. By U.S. standards, the benefits offered are low, and, although the protection costs $35 per year, it is projected that, if the plan were offered in urban areas of the United States with higher costs of living and salaries, its cost would multiply.

The other government experiment, under way in the Canadian province of Saskatchewan, is a plan in which no-fault and fault operate together. The Saskatchewan plan combines government and private insurance. The government runs the no-fault portion of the plan while the private insurance companies supplement it with liability coverage. This system has met with success in Saskatchewan, principally because of its low population density. It is open to debate whether a similar system could work as well in this country, especially in urban areas. As in Puerto Rico, the Saskatchewan plan keeps no-fault benefits relatively low, compared to what is offered by the Massachusetts or Keeton-O'Connell plan.

Government plans have several advantages over private insurance. Foremost is the ability to include all drivers, regardless of social and economic class, within its insurance scheme because of the government's ease in spreading risk. Also, advertising and marketing costs would be dramatically reduced. The obvious disadvantage of government intrusion into automobile insurance is the birth of a new bureaucracy to replace the private companies. Whether the addition of another federal agency in place of a service previously carried out by the private sector is desirable is always a controversial political issue. But, should private enterprise fail to deal effectively with the difficulties facing automobile insurance, the bureaucratic wall could be scaled.

Not surprisingly, the insurance industry has strongly resisted any government hand in automobile casualty insurance. Because it has feared federal regulation and ultimate takeover, the industry has been a firm advocate of state-by-state development. The ability to convince government to keep out is closely related to the future performance of no-fault. Without obvious gains to the insured, there will be growing pressure for a national government-operated no-fault package. By making insurance compulsory and abandoning fault, automobile insurance is moving closer to socialization.

But a more immediate danger is the enormous financial and political influence of the insurance industry that can be used to force poor plans such as the total no-fault proposal for New York upon the consuming public. Inspired by the profits made by companies in Massachusetts during 1971, they will be tempted to try. Advertising campaigns have been launched throughout the country on behalf of the major insurers arguing for a complete end to the fault system in automobile accidents. The industry's opinion-molding techniques have been imaginative, but the plans behind which it has stood are in neither the consumer's nor the victim's best interests.

8
Fault Reprieve

MOST OF THE EMPHASIS on automobile insurance reform has taken place on the no-fault front. In solving automobile insurance ills, state governments have seemingly eliminated from their strategy a serious look at improving the tort negligence system. Yet, thus far, states that have altered their methods of compensating accident victims are winding up with a combination of fault and no-fault. While the search for the ideal no-fault solution continues, it is equally important to repair what remains of the traditional liability structure.

As we have seen, the law of negligence originated as a by-product of the Industrial Revolution and was designed for the protection of defendants—the courts sought to confine entrepreneurial risk to those accidents where negligence could be shown. Vestiges of that desire to cut down the defendant's risk remain imbedded within the law today. In salvaging the fault system, the first step is to survey the law of negligence to eliminate the outworn but pervasive doctrines that are still in force. The second step is to modify the harsh impact of negligence law affecting the compensation of innocent victims. Third, we must re-evaluate the justifications for denying compensation to certain individuals. Finally, we must mold the three into an insurance program that minimizes waste and maximizes benefits to the accident victim.

At present, the law of negligence is littered with overly fine distinctions that hinder justice. With the development of the law of negligence through case-by-case decisions, the concept was broken down into rulings that reflect a nineteenth-century logic but do not always result in equitable benefit allowance for twentieth-century accident victims. It has been divided into a triangle of degrees: ordinary negligence, gross negligence, and willful, wanton, and reckless misconduct. Division of rights into these categories acts to exclude entire groups of injured motorists from any compensation at all.

Ordinary negligence we have defined earlier as the degree of care that a "reasonable man" is expected to exercise in a given situation. This standard is applied in driver-versus-driver situations. Both owe each other the obligation of exercising ordinary care, because they are coequal in status while using the public highway. This principle adapts well to automobile accidents.

There are persons on the highway who are not treated as equals. If the relationship is guest-host, the host is held to a lesser standard of care than in driver-versus-driver situations. In order for a guest to recover from his host, he must prove that his host was not only negligent but grossly negligent. Gross negligence is defined as the absence of that degree of care that even a careless man would exercise. This logic is based upon the inhospitable premise that you do not owe a guest very much regard for his safety, since you are doing him a favor. Because about one-third of all automobile accident injuries take place in single-car accidents—for example, a collision caused by a car hitting a tree—the retention of gross negligence as the standard for the guest-host relationship excludes all but a small handful of passengers who are injured in these one-car accidents. Passengers have been unable to collect against their own driver for their injuries, because it is extremely difficult to produce sufficient proof to establish this higher degree of fault.

The application of gross negligence to automobile accidents has survived with the blessing of the insurance industry. The industry opposed the elimination of this barrier because of its reluctance to increase the number of injured persons who could recover tort damages and because it feared collusion between host and guest to create fraudulent claim situations where the guest could successfully recover against the host's insurance company.

Withholding compensation to passengers by forcing them to prove gross negligence against their host is a serious flaw in the fault system. The cure is simple. Guest passengers ought to be allowed to recover tort damages through proof of ordinary negligence on the part of their hosts. Several states, following the lead of Wisconsin, have already eliminated the need to prove gross negligence in guest-passenger cases and have not created the problems projected by the industry.

The third side of the triangle requires the defendant to refrain from willful, wanton, and reckless misconduct. This standard is applied to those persons—such as trespassers—who are owed less care by the defendant than even under a guest-host relationship. Here the defendant is only required to avoid willfully, wantonly, or recklessly injuring such a person. Since very few automobile injuries fall within this third degree, this standard has little significance in automobile litigation.

Having cut down the degrees of negligence, we now turn to the necessity of eliminating some of the harsh defenses available to those who cause accidents. The defendant is generally going to be represented by his insurance company, which may be described as a "professional defendant" and as such has a large stake in perpetuating legal obstacles. The most unfair defense available is the doctrine of contributory negligence. Contributory negligence bars a plaintiff from all recovery, should he be found to have contributed even slightly to his own injury. Contributory negligence has been defined as the lack of that degree of care a reasonable man would exercise to provide for his own safety. Contributory negligence should be replaced with comparative negligence.

Comparative negligence allows an individual to recover damages proportional to his own degree of negligence. If it is determined that the victim contributed 25 per cent to his own injury, the plaintiff is compensated for 75 per cent of his total damages. Instead of being denied everything, the victim loses only a portion from his full recovery because of his own carelessness. But, if a person is more than 50 per cent responsible for his own accident, he is barred from all recovery. Contributory negligence works to bar the victim who contributes even 1 per cent to his own accident and is 99 per cent blameless. Had comparative negligence statutes been adopted sooner, the objection that the fault system excluded many deserving persons from recovery would not have been as valid as an argument in support of no-fault. As we saw, while Oregon and Massachusetts were enacting their no-fault reforms, they simultaneously enacted comparative negligence statutes.

Closely following modification of the degrees of negligence is the need to restructure the law of damages. The tort of negligence is divided into two components. Negligence must be shown, and, once that barrier is overcome, proof of damages must follow. Just as a softening of the law of negligence was suggested to broaden the number of individuals eligible for compensation, there is a necessity to update the law of damages. The objective is to pay more victims but in more precise relationship to the actual loss, thus eliminating the extravagances of the tort system.

At present, damages designed to compensate for lost wages are measured by the victim's loss of earning capacity. The law has shown a preference for loss of earning capacity over payment of actual lost wages; the distinction that has developed through a number of court decisions fixes recovery on the amount of compensation that could have been earned had the injured been able to work, instead of computing his out-of-pocket loss. The loss is paid as a potential rather than real loss. An accident victim will receive more money than if he had worked! Loss of earning capacity creates additional waste by returning gross earnings—wages payable before taxes, instead of net earnings. No-fault plans proposed to date take this overpayment into consideration by reimbursing 75–85 per cent of gross earnings.

The same saving could easily be adopted by the tort system to reduce its wage reparation costs. Suppose that a man is injured in an automobile accident and he is awarded damages. Under the laws of most states, if he were working and his earning capacity were $100 per week before taxes, he would be compensated for a full $100 per week. This happens even though his in-pocket income after taxes was $80 per week. Is there any justification for bestowing an additional $20 because he is an accident victim? Tort recovery is tax exempt. Even if he had been unemployed at the time of his accident, the victim would be compensated at the same rate upon proof that he was ready, willing, and able to work but could not do so because of his injury.

By paying for loss of earning capacity, there are numerous

situations in which double payments are made to accident
victims. This duplication results from the victim's receiving
funds from wage-continuation programs available at his job
as well as money from private collateral sources, such as insurance policies, in addition to tort payments for the same
damages. As we saw, the Massachusetts version of no-fault
tries to eliminate the double recovery of earnings by requiring the claimant to exhaust his private collateral resources
before looking to his no-fault policy. Because the accident
victim is forced to depend on his collateral resources for
damages that are legitimately within the province of automobile insurance, any cost reduction becomes an illusion.
The cost is transferred to activities other than automobile
accidents. In place of this, a corporation or insurance company that makes a voluntary or contractual payment to an
injured person for lost wages due to an automobile accident
should be reimbursed directly by the insurer as part of the
final adjustment of a claim. Re-allocating these funds from
automobile insurance by recycling them back into collatoral
wage sources is desirable under fault or no-fault as a way to
force the automobile to pay its own way.

This theory would work as follows: The automobile insurer, learning that the claimant received the payment of his
wages while incapacitated from a collateral source, would
be required to seek out the institution or individual paying
this money. A lien—a hold on claim proceeds for wage payments—would be used to refund the money obtained from
this source. The amount of the lien would be set off against
what was eventually recovered by the victim. Because the
double payment has placed an added burden on the cost
of automobile accidents, by permitting the injured to collect
twice for the same damage, ending double wage-recovery
would bring about a real gain.

Medical expenses is another weak area in the law of damages. At present, a victim is entitled to be compensated for the fair and reasonable amount of medical expense associated with his injury. No-fault has blindly followed this path without even a token attempt at changing this standard. Proposals such as the AIA plan call for payment of unlimited medical charges based upon the indefinite standard of the "fair and reasonable." Because some no-fault plans have tied the amount of a victim's medical bill to his right to be compensated for pain and suffering, a demand has been created for a fixed price list of medical services. For example, such routine procedures as examinations, suturing, and so forth could all be assigned a predetermined medical cost. Price and services rendered would be measured objectively. At the same time that accident benefits paid to victims are being drastically reduced and reformers are clamoring for the removal of legal fees from insurance costs, the medical profession has been given a blank check to charge whatever it deems reasonable and fair for its services.

The law needs changing and so do the methods by which the law is administered. The bar's lack of success in opposing the no-fault movement is in large measure due to media-stimulated disapproval of its stake in the perpetuation of the tort system. The contingent fee, exploited by the no-fault reformers, has called into question the bar's motivation in opposing no-fault and contributed to the bar's ineffectiveness in gaining support for its position.

The contingent fee was fostered by the idea that even the poorest man could afford the best lawyer if he did not have to pay him from his own pocket—the lawyer would wait until his case was decided, when he could pay. It was on this promise that lawyers were able to represent indigent clients. The plaintiff benefited from the contingent fee, because, if he were unsuccessful, he owed his attorney nothing. A better method of handling the contingent fee could be formulated. It is the policy of the American Trial Lawyers Association that every client be offered a choice of engaging a lawyer on a contingent-fee basis or on the basis of an hourly charge. The Cotter plan, originating in Connecticut and later adopted by Illinois, limits the amount of the contingent fee to 25 per cent. The Hart-Magnuson proposal for a national insurance system treats the problem of legal fees by restricting contingent fees to noneconomic recoveries; for economic losses, an hourly rate must be charged.

But the solution is not a legislative matter alone. The time has come for the American bar to recognize that ordinary lawsuits should not entail contingent fees in excess of one-third of the gross recovery. Fee arrangements should be reasonable. In setting the fee, careful consideration should be given to all factors, including the size of the recovery and the complexity of the lawsuit.

Aside from reform of existing laws of negligence and damages, any blueprint to upgrade the workings of the fault system must be accompanied by improvements in the court system itself. The existence of court congestion, regardless of its cause, is intolerable. In *Pinnick* v. *Cleary*, Justice Paul Reardon referred to automobile lawsuits as a "cancer in our court system." In some urban areas, a case may languish as long as five years on the docket before being brought to jury trial. The solution is not to deny individuals with legitimate disagreements access to impartial justice. Use of the judicial system cannot be forfeited for what is inexpensive or expedient.

One obvious solution is the appointment of more judges and the construction of more courtrooms, often obsolete and inadequate for the volume of business. As a social cost, it is far less expensive to expand the courts than abolish the right to use the court system for all except those litigants representing huge financial interests. Criminal law and corporate battles may someday be all that remains of the adversary system.

In addition, greater latitude must be given parajudicial court staff to deal effectively with the more routine court matters that burden the limited number of trial judges now on the bench. The staff of any clerk's office is competent to handle chores such as the call of the trial list, the handling of certain undisputed motions, requests for postponements, and so forth. The potential of parajudicial personnel has scarcely been tapped. Such people could be employed to advantage at the pretrial stage, to hear and sift through the issues and find areas of agreement, encourage settlement, and conserve the time spent on trials. Also, court schedules should be lengthened, and modern data processing techniques used to eliminate the administrative waste tied to old-fashioned compilation of records and documents.

Despite the original pleas for no-fault as a means of lifting the burdens on the courts, they can look forward to growing numbers of automobile cases; since states are heading toward dual fault–no-fault systems, lawsuit volume may be on the rise. No-fault plans split some claims into several pieces. An automobile accident that formerly resulted in one claim may now generate two or three separate lawsuits. To reduce court traffic significantly, the smaller claim must be eliminated entirely or made subject to compulsory arbitration. Plans such as Illinois has adopted, which have compulsory arbitration built into them, have taken a major step toward erasing the small claim from the docket. Compulsory arbitration of cases below $3,000 could result in a reduction of 80–90 per cent of the courts' automobile accident business. This step is not designed to deny any accident victim access to the courts, but only to provide a forum for quick and relatively informal hearings.

The courts are only one cause of delay in lawsuits. As U.S.

Supreme Court Chief Justice Warren Burger put it, "Lawyers are competitive creatures, and the adversary system encourages tension and often rewards delay." To counteract this, the plan used in the province of Ontario might be considered. When a defendant makes an attempt in good faith to settle a lawsuit, the offer is transmitted on a "payment into court" basis. If the plaintiff refuses the offer and is later totally unsuccessful or recovers a verdict less than the original offer, he is charged the defendant's costs of litigation. The plan is designed to create incentives for the parties to settle their disputes amicably, by making the failure to do so financially unattractive.

One of the often cited flaws in the fault system is delay in delivering benefits in the severe case, and an undue emphasis on all-at-one-time payments. Going back to the Oregon program, this defect has been solved by offering short-term economic benefits on a no-fault basis, later deducted from any lump-sum jury award or settlement based on fault. Again, this illustrates the fundamental compatibility of fault and no-fault.

Thus far, the legal and judicial sides of the issue have been under fire. Now we must look at the role of insurance in a system of law. To now, the mission of the law has been to identify and enforce legal rights and responsibilities. Insurance has served the function of providing indemnity for what the law was willing to compensate. With the introduction of no-fault principles, will the tail now be wagging the dog? We are asked to abandon fundamental ideas of fault and individual responsibility for a legal system more compatible with a decrease in the price of insurance. The question is raised as to whether what is in the best interest of the insurance industry will be ultimately best for the public.

Most of the complaints about the fault system have been generated by conditions spawned by the insurance industry.

The industry has allowed the quality of its service to decline to a point where it is no longer able to cope with accident volume. For years, companies demonstrated a devotion to outmoded claim-handling techniques as well as a lack of imagination in devising better ways to serve the public. For example, the industry did not use the telephone for investigation of automobile personal injury claims until well into the 1960's, when Liberty Mutual pioneered the end of the cumbersome method of personal contact insisted upon by claims departments. Settlement discussions were frequently conducted in a hostile way, which led to public condemnation of not only the insurance companies but the negligence system itself.

The record is replete with examples of underwriting blackouts in high-risk areas, insurance company bankruptcies, arbitrary cancellations, deceptive advertising practices, poor and dilatory claim handling, and take-it-or-leave-it settlement tactics. No-fault can do nothing to alter these factors if the industry itself is not willing to change. Changing the law of negligence will not result in any better performance unless a closer scrutiny by the licensing authorities results in effective changes. The state agencies must insist on action. The habitually poor performance of the insurers has become so intertwined with the public's general understanding of this system as to threaten the existence of the law of negligence. The tort system has been made the scapegoat of unfair practices, far beyond the scope and control of the law.

In any revised fault system, it is essential that the compensation of accident victims be broadened to include those who at present are denied effective recovery due to the lack or inadequacy of insurance coverage. Compulsory insurance or strictly enforced financial liability must be instituted at sufficient limits to compensate the seriously injured. Too

often the victim has been left holding a verdict that he
found impossible to convert to cash because there was no
insurance coverage to pay for it. Even where protection
against uninsured motorists is purchased, the limits are so
low that they are insufficient to help the victim with large-
scale damages. Yet the absence and inadequacy of personal
injury coverage is still being disregarded by most no-fault
reforms.

One mutually advantageous way law and insurance can
be wed is through merit-rating. Surveys show that motorists
overwhelmingly prefer to have the cost of their insurance
related to their own driving record. For merit-rating to be
meaningful, there must be mechanisms for assessing fault.
While no-fault proponents say that fault cannot be determined, the evidence is to the contrary. Accidents are caused
by driver error, and merit-rating is one way of fairly spreading the cost of insurance to those who cause accidents. But
merit-rating, on the basis of accident frequency alone, de-
feats its purpose. There must be a qualitative dimension
that takes fault into account.

Regardless of whether fault or no-fault prevails, another
look is required at the sometimes superficial categories set
up for rate-making purposes. These categories are based on
age, geographic location, occupation, and so forth. Often
they have nothing to do with individual merit. There are
instances in which insurance has been made prohibitively
expensive for the old, young, and culturally disadvantaged.
In the only year that Massachusetts attempted merit-rating,
there was a decrease in the total cost of automobile insurance premiums. Merit-rating was abandoned when the
insurance companies objected to the additional costs of score-
keeping necessary to keep track of chargeable demerits.

The law of negligence and insurance have also come together in a state automobile insurance proposal suggested

by John R. Jewell, the Insurance Commissioner of Maryland. After studying the various no-fault plans, the decision was made that the disadvantages of no-fault outweighed its advantages. Abandoning the possibility of no-fault, Jewell came up with the "pay as you drive" plan, a state-operated program that would transfer a portion of automobile insurance from the private companies to a state agency. The plan combines social and private insurance. If the driver wants excess coverage, the plan assumes that, just as in the Puerto Rico and Saskatchewan plans, the private companies will supplement the minimum state coverage. Its announced goal would be the elimination of the vexations and discriminatory cancellations on motor vehicle insurance. No one in Maryland could have his insurance canceled if his car was duly registered.

The Maryland plan is an effort to relate the cost of insurance to those who drive on the roads and directly cause the losses, eliminating the overly generalized rating categories that lumped individual drivers into groups. Insurance premiums would be rated entirely on the personal driving record of each car-owner. As accidents and driving records would be inseparably linked, the object would be to bring to life again the incentive to drive safely. The deterrent would not be a potential lawsuit but an increase in the cost of purchasing automobile insurance. The attainment of the highest premium level would result in automatic loss of license. The Maryland plan is a total plan that includes as well a program for upgrading road safety and law enforcement, all within the same administrative framework.

Maryland has formulated an unusual method for paying for this protection. Unlike premiums paid to a private company, there would be no single premium payments. The Maryland plan would be funded by a surcharge on the purchase of license plates, which are a precondition to driving an automobile, fees from the purchase and renewal of driver's licenses, and a premium of two cents per gallon placed upon gasoline purchased in the state.

The "pay as you drive" program, although untested, makes a good deal of sense. It takes into account the responsibility for the high cost of insurance, placing it upon those who use the roads more than others. Insurance is connected to the model and size of automobiles, with the owners of those that have greater horsepower and that use more gasoline paying more. This may encourage the purchase of smaller, less powerful cars as an added safety incentive. Also the price of insurance is paid at increasing levels in small painless installments. The Maryland plan retains the tort system, which fits in comfortably with its merit-rating reform. While automobile insurance rating has been growing more impersonal elsewhere, Maryland has made an effort to tie the cost of driving to the individual.

Although the no-fault proponents have gone to great lengths to demonstrate the futility of locating fault in automobile accidents, Massachusetts in 1969 alone recorded over 200,000 moving motor vehicle violations, including speeding, driving so as to endanger life or property, driving under the influence of alcohol, and other clear-cut acts of highway irresponsibility. Is it possible to deny that an individual who ignores a stop sign and causes serious injury should not be held morally and legally responsible for the damages he causes? Another way of making that individual pay for his carelessness is to deny him recovery from benefits available from a tort system. In 1969, over 60,000 automobile-related deaths occurred, of which 30,000 were directly attributable to the use of alcohol. We come back to a sharp disagreement with Keeton and O'Connell, who would dismiss the concept of moral fault as irrelevant in automobile accident compensation.

Fault Reprieve

Fault Reprieve 139

The effort here has been to bring the law of negligence into harmony with current social trends. Those who are convinced that the fault system has a place in the future of automobile insurance law must insist that the rights of innocent victims be protected. Far from being at the end of of the road, the tort system has a long and challenging way to go. The law of negligence is not dead or even dying, but it has been asleep for a long time. The adversary system can no longer stand still and expect to survive the effort to substitute cheap insurance for equity.

9
At the Nation's Capitol

DURING THE MID-1960's, the growing dissatisfaction with automobile insurance found a sympathetic ear in Washington. Complaints poured into congressional offices and, as a result of consumer demands for investigation, Congress mandated that the Department of Transportation undertake a study of the entire automobile insurance system. The final report, a massive twenty-three volumes, looks into every facet, ranging from public attitudes toward automobile insurance practices to government regulation of the industry. Drawing upon these studies, DOT, in March of 1971, came out with a final report, a blueprint for automobile insurance reform, calling for first-party insurance and no-fault.

The automobile insurance battle is opening a second front. In addition to fault versus no-fault, the latest issue is state versus federal control. The DOT report is clearly in favor of reform on a state-by-state basis and urges that each state take on a cautious attitude, so that warning signs on the virtues and shortcomings of the new no-fault systems can be heeded and reform stopped and redirected where necessary. A national plan administered by a new federal agency is not considered. The department favors a state-regulated no-fault first-party coverage to provide compensation for economic losses of all descriptions. Cost reduction for the consumer is achieved by the emphasis on coordination of benefits, the use of deductibles that make the victim a self-insurer, and the termination of the adversary system as the principal method of determining who will receive automobile insurance compensation. The right to sue is retained for only the most severe cases.

The DOT report was greatly influenced by consumer complaints about the performance of insurance companies in an adversary system. With a first-party system, the driver would no longer have to leave to chance which insurance company he would turn to in the event of an accident. DOT argued it would improve the relationship between consumer and company because of the more direct, personal relationship created by first-party coverage.

The DOT report opted for a first-party plan, having another disadvantage of fault-finding in mind: that the company, in agreeing to insure, would be in a better position to evaluate the risk it was assuming. Under a third-party adversary system, the only measure in rating used was the likelihood of a risk to cause accidents. With more personal information available about a potential victim, the company would be able to target its risks closely.

Rating criteria, which have irritated the public for years and have been responsible to a large extent for the widespread dissatisfaction with automobile insurance, will be revised. The department realizes that the motoring public is especially irate with the industry's practice of whimsical cancelations and high rates. It is predicted—bitter argument notwithstanding—that there will be a narrowing of the chasm that now exists between the extremes of rate classifications. As we have seen, automobile insurance will become readily available to those who at the present time are considered undesirable risks.

These points, though important, are secondary. A recurring theme in the fault–no-fault controversy is whether or not there is a moral obligation for society to extend benefits to all traffic victims, regardless of their conduct in contributing toward their own misfortune: Is this the task of a socially responsible system of insurance? DOT believes that all motorists' economic losses should be covered regardless of fault, including medical expense, wage loss, and property damage, though it does not go as far as the AIA plan in making these benefits unlimited. Instead, it suggests that optional coverage be made available to motorists by the insurance industry to protect against the most catastrophic losses. It prefers to allow the individual the choice of absorbing his own smaller losses by liberal use of deductibles.

Greater coordination of benefits from automobile insurance with other resources was another guideline laid down by the Department of Transportation. As we have seen, the system is burdened by competing and overlapping forms of coverage from both the government—social security protection, welfare, the proposed national health insurance plan —and private insurance plans such as Blue Cross and Blue Shield. DOT recommends that all government insurance coverage ought to be primary, used even before automobile insurance. In the absence of some applicable social insurance plan, automobile coverage then would be used prior to all other private collateral health insurance sources. Duplicate medical coverages should be allowed only with the prior knowledge and consent of insurer and insured.

On the issue of private versus public insurance, the study

took a firm stand, expressing a preference for private insurance plans until they demonstrated beyond doubt that they could no longer function efficiently. It suggests that small amounts of compulsory insurance be used to induce the consumer to purchase more than the minimum needed to assure his own protection. This stems from a desire to keep the base price for this insurance low, thus avoiding pressure for a public takeover. But the idea appears contradictory, because if the DOT plan were instituted benefits would be meager, the costs high, and the opportunity for general damages totally eliminated. If the level of compulsion to purchase insurance as advocated by the study remained low, those in the worst economic positions would be forced to absorb the greatest portion of their own losses. Low minimum requirements for insuring a car under compulsory insurance may imply low cost, but the real consequence would be low benefits, as happened in Massachusetts.

The study goes on at length about the need to make available additional supplementary coverage, but on a noncompulsory basis. It is impossible to imagine the so-called nonstandard market—an insurance euphemism for poor people—voluntarily buying any of these additional coverages, because the basic costs at present of automobile purchase, maintenance, and insurance are assumed with difficulty. The DOT case against forcing people to buy more coverage is that it might lead to pressures for greater governmental takeover of the private insurance field. Advocates of such a takeover contend that first-party no-fault insurance could be administered more economically by the government, returning the profit and marketing expense consumed by private insurance to the motorist. Sales commissions alone exceed 10 per cent of the total cost of automobile insurance.

The DOT study maintains the use of the adversary system as the method for awarding general and intangible damages, including pain and suffering. It has not been determined if a first-party system guaranteeing payment to all victims injured in automobile accidents will have sufficient money left to supply claims for general damage. The availability of money remaining to compensate these kinds of claims will hinge upon whether the no-fault limits are placed high or low. If a low level of no-fault compulsion is maintained, as DOT suggests, there will be more room in the system for general damage awards. Because more individuals will be made eligible to become successful claimants and benefits in some circumstances will be improved, it is openly acknowledged by DOT that the transition to first-party no-fault coverage from a tort system may in fact increase the price of insurance.

Where the use of fault is retained, the department insists on a high though unspecified medical threshold before a victim may make a fault claim for pain and suffering. No objective standards are offered to help draw the line.

In addition to permitting claims for pain and suffering where the medical bill exceeds a predetermined threshold, the study suggests that intangible losses be recoverable in cases of permanent loss of function or disfigurement. Similar to the Massachusetts-Florida solution, it tacitly acknowledges that compensation for only economic losses is inequitable, particularly in severe cases. A permanent injury to a vital function, a significant and embarrassing disfigurement, or serious emotional upset should not be overlooked. The department is confident from its polling that the public is willing to forgo general damages in smaller cases in exchange for a reduction of insurance premium cost. But the validity of this conclusion can only be tested if there is agreement upon the ultimate definition of what constitutes a small case.

The DOT blueprint recommends generous payments for

loss of income. In an effort to discourage the small claim, a waiting period is advised before wage protection payments are made. The department calls for a ceiling of $1,000 per person per month to be included as part of a compulsory package, accompanied by an option to purchase higher limits for those who feel their earning capacity requires greater protection. Loss of income protection is expected to complement the opportunity for rehabilitation, and the protection will be offered during rehabilitation even if an accident involves an injury that in no way interferes with an individual's employment. Wage continuation is given a three-year limit with benefits pegged at $1,000 per month or a maximum total of $36,000. More coverage may be purchased at the insured's option. As in the other no-fault bills, the department's includes a provision for hiring substitute services at $75 per week.

The department study further urges the implementation of compulsory no-fault property damage insurance. It stresses the opportunity for premium savings by the use of deductibles. The ideal would be for the accident victim to turn to his own company for all the consequences of his accident, including personal injuries and property damage with the exception of claims for pain and suffering, which would remain part of the adversary system. By employing deductibles and self-insuring for a substantial part of the damage to one's own car, the cost of insurance is again reduced.

The DOT report points toward a predicted savings from group marketing of no-fault automobile insurance. According to DOT, employee associations, unions, and fraternal and religious groups can now band together to purchase automobile insurance as a block, cutting down costs for the participant by the company offering a discount. DOT recognizes that this market trend promises savings to some but potentially could add to the cost of automobile insurance for those who are not included in a group.

The DOT study is the first of many expected federal incursions into the automobile insurance field. The McCarran-Ferguson Act, passed by Congress in 1944, has left the regulation of the insurance companies exclusively to the states. The industry has prospered under the shield of laissez-faire. With increased recognition that automobile insurance is an interstate problem, the outcry for federal regulation is going to become louder. And, with greater reliance on compulsory insurance, the private insurance companies are sure to face a future of tighter regulation by state or federal government.

The private insurance companies will have to be more closely watched as to the amount of profits they should be allowed to retain from compulsory insurance. Where excess profits above a statutory maximum are achieved, any compulsory insurance plan, be it first-party no-fault or third-party fault, must provide a statutory rebate to the consumer. Investment profits and losses under a compulsory system should be considered as part of the rate as well. To reduce price, rate-setting by prior approval must give way to open competition among the companies.

At present, DOT sees its role as advisory rather than legislative. After each state has complied with the guidelines, DOT would try to reconcile all the various state plans to encourage a reasonable degree of national uniformity. But it warns against a commitment to a national pattern without detailed observation of the states that have already passed no-fault plans.

For the first phase, it is urged that medical costs be paid on a no-fault basis. At the same time, the right to sue for intangible damages in nearly all cases would be eliminated. Before this is brought about, an in-depth estimate of cost-savings must be constructed, so that the price of automobile insurance, in the absence of any real experience with this type of experimental coverage, will not be made unduly high. The second phase would be the introduction of a wage-continuation program, substitute-help provisions, and payment of funeral costs. Finally, property damage claims would be added to the first-party system. When these three stages are completed, automobile insurance will be operated on a totally no-fault first-party method. In order to institute the DOT program, a five-year testing period is suggested to enable public policy-makers to react to the various phases and developments of the incremental steps.

Whether or not the federal government has the constitutional right to impose its guidelines over automobile insurance, which the states regard as their domain, remains to be decided. When the Massachusetts Supreme Court considered the constitutionality of its no-fault insurance reform, it relied upon the constitutional grant of power of a state to control automobile insurance through its police power. The DOT saw the power over automobile insurance as resting with the national government, based upon federal control over interstate commerce. If that power does exist—and it is likely that it does, because automobile insurance has an undeniable impact on interstate commerce—the case of *Pinnick* v. *Cleary*, decided on the premise that the state has the right to control automobile insurance, may be open to further inquiry.

In summary, the department has high hopes that a no-fault system will grant certainty in the availability and amount of payment for accident victims, eliminate delays inherent in the adversary process, and close the gap between actual economic losses and payments in fact received by the victims. The department insists that its reform suggestions will result in better allocation of the benefits of automobile insurance. It seeks to narrow the disparity of recovery by paying for all kinds of economic losses. Because all economic losses are designed to be paid promptly and completely, and because pain and suffering payments have been virtually eliminated, the reasons that might have existed under the tort system to maximize damages in order to increase rewards will no longer exist. But to announce the end of general damages because of uncontrollable fraud is to acknowledge that no reasonable form of insurance will work. Nevertheless, DOT has thrown its hat into the no-fault ring and with these selling points seeks to convert the states to its program.

Hard on the heels of the DOT report, a bill was sponsored jointly in the U.S. Senate by Senators Philip Hart of Michigan and Warren Magnuson of Washington; it is the first to outline a complete national first-party no-fault insurance program. The Hart-Magnuson proposal includes restructuring of both personal injury and property damage protection. First-party no-fault would become compulsory insurance on a national scale to all users and owners of automobiles.

Every insurer who is authorized to write automobile insurance under this plan is compelled to offer a noncancelable insurance policy binding the insurer to the insured, except in cases of nonpayment of premiums or revocation of the insured's driver's license, which Hart believes are the only two legitimate excuses for refusing to sell automobile insurance. Discriminatory classifications with higher rates to bartenders or waitresses because they were considered "lower breed" or for priests because of a "Lord will protect me attitude" first led Hart, through his interest in civil rights, to automobile insurance reform. The subsequent failure to supply an insurance product to large sectors of the market caused him to press for change.

The inclusion of a noncancelability clause is a direct

attempt to end the paradox of legislating compulsory insurance while allowing the companies the option of denying insurance to potential customers. A similar clause introduced into the Massachusetts no-fault bill caused the insurance companies to threaten to cease writing in Massachusetts; it took a subsequent legislative amendment to convince the insurers that they ought to remain. The Hart-Magnuson noncancelability feature is the strongest of its type ever advocated in automobile insurance.

Hart-Magnuson would pay all medical and rehabilitation costs. These expenses would be open-ended and not subject to any restriction other than they be appropriate and reasonable. The plan would guarantee payment of net lost wages and reimbursement for impairment of earning capacity less deductions for taxes, until there is complete physical recovery. A limitation of $1,000 per month is placed on the wage provision, with a mandatory option to purchase more protection, if desired. An allowance for the hiring of substitute help is also included. These measures are consistent with the DOT recommendations.

The property damage section of the plan provides payment for all property damage caused to the insured's automobile regardless of fault. If a parked car were struck, the claim would be made against the company of the driver striking it. If a moving car were struck, each driver would make claim for property damage payment to his own insurance policy.

To replace the benefits swept away by the switch to no-fault, Hart-Magnuson offers two options designed to make available to the accident victim the same rights to compensation that exist at the present time for the successful plaintiff. The first option pays for economic losses above the no-fault limits. This would rarely be used, because the no-fault largesse is broad. The second option pays for general damages, including pain and suffering. As a precondition to collecting under either option, the victim must prove fault by the driver causing the injury. The availability of these options allows free competition between choice of fault or no-fault compensation.

Unlike most no-fault plans, the Hart-Magnuson optional personal injury coverages require no minimum threshold, such as Massachusetts's $500 medical bill or Keeton-O'Connell's $10,000 economic loss, before a claim for pain and suffering can be pursued. Professor Alfred Conard of the University of Michigan Law School, commenting on the possible purchase of this type of optional choice, doubts that anyone will voluntarily purchase it. Without any projections as to what the cost of this coverage might be, it is impossible to predict its acceptability. The high point of Hart-Magnuson—retaining all benefits currently available under the fault system in full—is a mirage until price is pinpointed.

Hart-Magnuson's reliance upon pain-and-suffering options based upon fault is inspired by the newest version of Keeton-O'Connell, which also supplements no-fault with options. It represents a shift in strategy by the no-fault advocates. Instead of insisting on outright annihilation of general damages claims, they are now seeking to price them out of existence. This type of coverage in practice should work similarly to the present coverage called "uninsured motorists protection." In this plan, a policyholder, finding his adversary uninsured, assumes the role of plaintiff against his own company. To be paid, he must prove that his injuries were the product of the uninsured driver's negligence and that he, the insured, was not guilty of contributory negligence. In addition, the policyholder is subject to contractual defenses, such as failure to cooperate or failure to give proper notice, that do not exist in the tort system.

This kind of optional coverage is discriminatory, because only those who are in a position to afford it will be protected against losses due to intangible damages. The price can be expected to be high. This means that the poorer segments of the driving public will lose an entire range of funda- mental rights to be fully compensated for personal injuries. It is a rich man's law—his economic losses are higher, and buying the options is not a financial hardship.

One feature built into this plan gives rise to an "equal protection" problem similar to that raised in *Pinnick* v. *Cleary*. Persons injured in automobile accidents who are passengers or pedestrians and have had no opportunity, as either an insured or a dependent of an insured, to purchase optional coverage for economic losses above the minimum limits or for pain and suffering are permitted to recover their full damages in an action of tort, just as if this national no-fault act had not been passed. Children of parents with- out motor vehicles retain the right to sue for pain and suf- fering, while children whose parents own an automobile do not. Individuals have been unfairly divided into distinct categories that afford differing rights and privileges.

Unlike Keeton-O'Connell, Hart-Magnuson does not feed on the victim's collateral resources to reduce the cost of in- surance. This proposal allows the victim to keep all benefits from other sources, except those derived from public assis- tance. In this way, the motorist is allowed flexibility in making his automobile coverage compatible with other forms of duplicate protection. By tailoring the total insur- ance program, a cost-saving is achieved. The exclusion of double payments where public money is obtained is an attempt to blend national health insurance, when it is passed, with national no-fault automobile insurance.

Again differing from most no-fault plans, Hart-Magnuson does not depend on arbitration as a replacement for the courts. There are many occasions when the right to bring suit, particularly where the insured purchases the pain-and-suffering option, can be exercised.

In the plan, there is a curious twist to the payment of legal fees. If the dispute is over compulsory no-fault coverage, the insurance company pays its insured's lawyer even if the company wins, unless the suit is fraudulent or not brought in good faith. The plan ignores the overworked no-fault argument that elimination of court congestion is a legitimate reason for abolishing basic rights. This scheme *does* keep the courthouse door open to accident victims who can afford the optional coverages or who run afoul of their insurance company.

The Hart-Magnuson plan calls for federal no-fault automobile insurance. It refuses to follow the Department of Transportation's guideline that each state develop its own system of no-fault insurance, as long as it is generally compatible with common no-fault objectives. Hart-Magnuson believes that the states cannot or will not go to a true no-fault plan.

Throughout its history, the automobile insurance industry has successfully resisted federally imposed standards. Because of the DOT report and Hart-Magnuson, the states may find the companies, under the threat of national regulation, coming forward with innovative suggestions of their own. But should the Hart-Magnuson method of reform become law, the federal government will regulate automobile insurance for the first time. And on the Washington horizon is an all-encompassing federal system of health insurance regulated and controlled by the government.

The Nixon Administration has gone on record as favoring the concept of no-fault insurance. Department of Transportation Secretary John Volpe has openly embraced the

formula for automobile insurance reform drawn up by
Keeton-O'Connell. So far, the administration has backed
the DOT endorsement of a gradual changeover to no-fault
by the individual states. DOT guidelines notwithstanding,
it is probable that many years will pass before each state
adopts a no-fault approach that satisfies the federal government. Several states that have converted to partial no-fault
packages—including Oregon, Delaware, Illinois, and South
Dakota—have done so with plans that are unrelated to those
suggested by the department. The greatest strength of the
department's approach is its commitment to gradualness.
This will give rival reforms, such as that proposed for
Maryland, an opportunity to compete with radical no-fault.

In view of state-by-state reform, it is unlikely that sufficient support will exist in Congress for the passage of the
Hart-Magnuson federal plan. It faces the combined opposition of the administration, the insurance industry, the American Trial Lawyers Association, and the proponents of other
methods of reform. But failure of the states to devise a win-
ning game plan for automobile insurance reform would go
far to create the climate for congressional action on a nationwide plan.

10

Cost or Equity?

As THE DRIVE to institute no-fault reform continues across the country, the prospect of immediate consumer savings has been relentlessly paraded before the public. It is generally agreed that, if a 15 per cent reduction in compulsory insurance had not been attached to the Massachusetts legislation, no-fault would not have passed. To combat this appeal, those who are convinced that the fault system should be retained and improved face an uphill fight. Regardless of how efficiently or inexpensively the fault system can be made to operate, it can never challenge no-fault on a cost basis, for a fundamental reason. No-fault is able to expand or contract benefits at will and, therefore, control costs as its designers see fit.

The price of liability insurance under a fault system is determined by the law dictating the risk—what claims will be paid and how much. Insurance costs are controlled by external factors, the risk the law imposes. No-fault, by permitting the insurance industry to break away from its traditional function of paying losses recognized by law, exchanges established legal rights for a neatly packaged insurance risk. The law of negligence is displaced by the law of the insurance industry, and we find the wolf left to guard the sheep.

The price of no-fault insurance is further controlled by making it compulsory. While no-fault maximizes the contribution into the pool, it carefully regulates the benefits that can be returned to the victim. If every person injured in an automobile accident were to be paid by no-fault to the same extent that innocent victims are compensated under the present tort system, a doubling or tripling in price might well follow.

Because of its need to keep costs attractively low to maintain its competitive price advantage, payments are typically controlled in no-fault plans by eliminating or reducing claims for general and intangible damages, including pain and suffering, disfigurement, and so forth; paying wage losses fractionally, rather than wholly; relying on the victim's personal collateral resources; and inducing the purchaser to self-insure by offering deductibles. What appears to be a cost-saving is in reality a cost-shifting. The promised cost reduction is part of a shell game, and the public has been encouraged to look under the wrong shell. In every case, the benefits taken away from innocent victims are exceeded by even the most optimistic cost-savings. In Massachusetts, for example, although compulsory personal injury insurance was reduced by 15 per cent, measured against the previous year, the amount of money paid to all accident victims was down by over 70 per cent.

Without cost reduction, no-fault can never expect to command popular support. It has been advertised as an "everybody gets paid–low cost" program, but with no catch phrase on the value of lost benefits. Just as a $10,000 life insurance

policy costs more than a $1,000 policy, the same logic ap-
plies to no-fault. As Professor David Sargent of Suffolk University Law School has said, "The cheapest insurance is
no insurance at all."

Automobile insurance based on negligence never intended
to pay all victims of all accidents. It recognized the need to
make value judgments to seek out the innocent. Because
the search for this qualitative justice requires time and
money, by compensating only worthy accident victims fully
and fairly the fault system is put at a superficial cost disadvantage. No-fault seizes on the cost of this search, saying
that, if it were abandoned, the funds could be put back
into the insurance pool for everyone's good. But, when this
money is not spent, the innocent victim is left decidedly
worse off than he was under fault.

Actuaries predict that each person living in the United
States will be involved in three traffic accidents in his life-
time. Year after year, most of these potential victims will
purchase automobile insurance. Perhaps because people
pay their insurance premiums annually and yet, on the
average, have accidents far less frequently, they tend to
think of themselves primarily as purchasers of insurance
and not potential victims, an idea much encouraged by
insurance industry no-fault advertising. This savings illusion is shattered only when the consumer finds himself in a
smashup. The ideal system of automobile insurance has yet
to be devised. Any total solution would certainly retain the
best features of negligence and harmonize these features
with long overdue improvements in casualty insurance.

Because complaints about automobile insurance are national in scope and deal with underwriting and regulatory
practices that can be best controlled by the federal government, the government should take the lead. As a first step, it
should end the exemption from federal intervention granted

the automobile insurance industry by the McCarran-Ferguson Act. Standardization of rating criteria, greater attention to consumer complaints, and insurance for all are but a few of the measures than can be brought about with the help of Congress.

Unfortunately, reform proposals to date have concerned reduced insurance costs, diverting attention from more critical problems. What has been missing on the part of the reformers is a genuine effort to take the less spectacular steps necessary to preserve what is equitable in our system of justice. We have been encouraged to abandon the use of the adversary system for a no-fault system in which insurance companies are subject only to the control of regulatory commissions, which have already demonstrated they are incapable of exercising effective restraints over the companies. We are asked to forgo adjudication and leave accident reparation entirely in the hands of the architects of no-fault bills.

Meaningful reform must be preceded by public understanding of the roles of the players—the industry, the bar, and the government. Attractive merchandising has distorted the objectives of the reformers. Is it true that you are in "good hands" with Allstate? Will Liberty Mutual really "stand by you"? As in many other areas in American life, advertising has run ahead of the product; expectation is not fulfilled by reality. The overwhelming number of complaints about the fault system received by DOT have dealt with insurance company practices. And yet the companies are now about to be rewarded with a financial bonanza by a changeover to no-fault.

The bar's position has been undermined both from within and without. The DOT study shows that plaintiff attorney fees amount to about 6.4 per cent of the total premiums referred to by the no-fault reformers. The total cost of lawyers' fees for both the plaintiff and defendant will not exceed the price of the agents' commission for selling and renewing year after year what is now compulsory insurance. The caricature of the negligence lawyer as a fee-crazed ambulance chaser has been overworked by critics of the bar. The function of the negligence bar has been to represent people who are victims of misfortune and assist them in their efforts to compete with superior economic interests. Now we find the image of the trial lawyers tarnished by the campaign to discredit the fault system. Thus far, the bar has been ineffective in its counterattack. In order to gain credibility with the public, it must convince the public that it is prepared to limit the contingent fee to a reasonable amount and that the client be given the choice of being represented on an hourly charge basis. Until this occurs, the bar is vulnerable to the charge that its concern with the preservation of tort law in automobile accidents is motivated solely by greed. It is also imperative that the bar seize the initiative to refine and improve the fault system itself.

State governments must also be made to meet their responsibilities. Too often, insurance commissions have not adequately regulated the companies. But often politicians have opted for the expedient short-range, instead of the more difficult long-range, solution. This is what happened in Massachusetts, and it can happen elsewhere. Politicians are never happier than when they can announce that their constituents are going to save money.

On the national front, no-fault will do nothing to end the carnage on our highways, which continue to be unsafe, overcrowded, poorly designed, and devoid of enthusiastic law enforcement. We have so far failed to devise acceptable alternatives to the automobile for moving people from place to place. A national mass-transit system would do more permanent good than a freeway stacked bumper to bumper with automobile insurance reforms. The costs of accident insurance will be automatically decreased if Congress takes the lead by providing suitable alternatives to the automobile. Encouraging the automobile by offering insurance at prices that do not reflect the true amount of damage it inflicts works counter to the goals of protecting the individual and the environment.

Despite Congressional action in the field of automobile safety, automobiles are still rolling in from Detroit, grotesquely overpowered and structually unsound. Tests show that these cars damage easily and are inadequately designed to withstand even slight impact, leaving the occupants dangerously unprotected. Even safety equipment, shoulder harnesses, and seat belts have been improperly designed and need improvement and uniform standards. Meaningful cost reduction in insurance must start not only with a reduction in accident frequency, but also with fewer human and material losses resulting from the accidents that will continue to occur.

What is needed in automobile insurance reform is not spectacular change but quiet evolution. As Chief Justice Tauro of the Massachusetts Supreme Judical Court said, "Let us not burn down the barn to get rid of the mice." Those who are fighting to preserve the negligence system must become as zealous as those who wish to end it. It has been an easy decision for legislators to jump on the no-fault bandwagon. The compulsion to do something, do anything but do it now, must be halted in Congress and the state legislatures at the insistence of a well-informed electorate. The whole story has yet to be told. A bread-and-circuses approach will not produce sensible reform.

Far-reaching implications in abandoning the fault system have been overlooked in the public debate. Aside from the monetary benefits lost, there is a radical departure from the insistence upon individual responsibility. At a time when individual rights are being defined and defended in areas such as consumer protection, the environment, free speech, and the treatment of defendants in criminal cases, the rights and duties of civil litigants have been swept under the rug. If it is unjust to take away from the innocent and give to the guilty, it is inconsistent to permit the irresponsible driver to put his hand in the pocket of his victim to share equally in compensation for the same accident. The body count from automobile accidents has been so awesome that there must be a personal accounting by the individual drivers responsible. No social or moral advantage is gained by eliminating the deterrent of having the careless driver know in advance that he cannot recover anything for his damages when he is at fault.

Insurance of the future will combine fault and no-fault. No-fault has distinct advantages as a secondary form of protection used to get benefits to the accident victim when he is in greatest need—while the injury is in the early stages of treatment. No-fault can end the hardship of delay as well as the uncertainties brought about by dependence on a lump-sum settlement. But the danger is that its usefulness will be oversold. The proper role of no-fault should be supplementary; it must not be a cornerstone of an entirely new legal system.

Because the application of no-fault benefits is a form of social insurance, it should be administered by the state. Judging from the successful performance of state-operated workmen's compensation funds, the state is able to run this type of insurance more cost-efficiently than the private sector. As a bonus, the need to make a profit is eliminated. Let the government operate no-fault as social insurance and the private companies continue with liability coverage. This coverage would be compatible with the various proposed national health insurance programs, and could be operated by an existing government agency, such as DOT or the Social Security Administration, or by an entirely new agency.

Regardless of whether the state or private companies administer the new automobile insurance, a middle ground has yet to be found that can include fault and no-fault techniques. The initial, most important step is to determine fairly the optimum combination of cost to the consumer and equity to the victim. But for those struggling to reach that meeting place safely, the hyperbole and hysteria characteristic of the current automobile insurance debate must first come to a quick halt.

Index